REAL ESTATE IS NOT FOR EVERYONE

REAL ESTATE IS NOT FOR EVERYONE

GABRIEL PALOTAS

Gabriel Palotas
Real Estate Is Not For Everyone

Published by Spines Publishing Platform
ISBN: 979-8-89950-320-7

Spines

CONTENTS

REAL ESTATE IS NOT FOR EVERYONE

BY GABRIEL PALOTAS

The saying "when one door closes, another opens" is a proverb that suggests that when a specific opportunity or path is closed, new opportunities or paths will inevitably emerge. It encourages optimism and resilience in the face of setbacks, reminding individuals to look beyond the closed door and see the new possibilities that are available.

The proverb's meaning is rooted in the idea that life is full of change and that disappointments or failures can pave the way for better outcomes. It suggests that even though a particular door may be closed, there are always other doors that are open to us, and we should focus on finding them. An example of using this proverb after losing a job, expressing that while disappointed, they know other opportunities will arise.

FRONT MATTER

This book is dedicated to those who dare to question the status quo, seek a life of purpose and freedom, and believe that happiness doesn't always come with a mortgage payment. It is dedicated to the dreamers, adventurers, and unconventional thinkers who are forging their paths to a fulfilling and financially secure life.

The world is constantly changing, and so are our priorities. What used to be considered a cornerstone of financial security—owning a home—is now being challenged by a new generation that values flexibility, freedom, and experiences over traditional markers of success.

This book reflects that shift. It's a guide for anyone who wants to break free from the confines of conventional wisdom and explore alternative ways to live a happy and fulfilling life.

We will delve into the complexities of homeownership, examining the hidden costs and potential downsides that often go unnoticed. We will also explore the liberating benefits of renting, the allure of alternative lifestyles, and the beauty of embracing a life less ordinary.

This book is not about telling you what to do, but rather empowering you with the knowledge and tools to make informed decisions about your housing choices and future. We will examine the financial implications, the emotional rewards, and the endless possibilities that lie beyond the traditional path.

So, if you're ready to challenge the norm, embrace adventure, and redefine what success truly means, join us on this journey. This book is for you.

The American Dream—a phrase that evokes images of picket fences, manicured lawns, and the comfort of owning a home. For decades, this dream has been ingrained in our collective consciousness, fueling a cultural obsession with homeownership. But what if that dream is no longer serving us?

In today's world, with ever-changing career paths, increasing job mobility, and a growing desire for experiences over possessions, the traditional path to homeownership may not be the best choice for everyone.

This book challenges the conventional wisdom and explores the complexities of housing choices in a way that is both honest and empowering. We will examine the true cost of homeownership, dissecting the often-overlooked expenses and potential downsides. We will then explore the liberating benefits of renting, the allure of alternative lifestyles, and the freedom that comes with embracing a life less ordinary. Whether you are a young professional starting out, a retiree looking to downsize, or a family seeking the best environment for your children, this book will provide the knowledge and insights you need to make informed decisions about your future. We will delve into the practicalities of finding the best places to live, considering factors like cost of living, safety, education, and healthcare. We will also explore the growing trend of living abroad, examining the opportunities and challenges of relocating to countries with a lower cost of living.

Throughout this journey, we will emphasize the importance of financial literacy and empower you to make choices that align with your values and goals. This is a book about more than just housing; it's about reclaiming your freedom, embracing your potential, and living a life that truly resonates with you.

THE CHALLENGES OF HOME OWNERSHIP

1

THE HIDDEN COSTS OF HOMEOWNERSHIP

Imagine this: You've just signed the dotted line, keys in hand, and the exhilarating feeling of homeownership washes over you. You're finally stepping into a place you can truly call your own. But as the initial excitement subsides, a sobering realization sets in: the mortgage. This behemoth of a financial commitment, while initially exciting, can quickly become a constant presence in your life.

Mortgages are the bedrock of homeownership, often the largest financial undertaking in a person's life. They are long-term loans that allow you to purchase a home, with regular payments made to gradually pay off the principal and interest over time. The mortgage payment is the lifeblood of your homeownership journey, and understanding its intricacies is crucial to navigating the financial landscape ahead.

Let's break down the components of this often-misunderstood element of homeownership.

The Anatomy of a Mortgage Payment

Your mortgage payment is not a single, monolithic sum. It's a carefully calculated cocktail of different components, each playing a significant role in determining your overall financial burden.

Principal: This is the actual amount you borrowed to purchase the home. With each payment, a portion goes towards reducing this principal amount, bringing you closer to owning your home outright.

Interest: The cost of borrowing money. Think of it as the price you pay for having the luxury of borrowing money to buy your home. This interest rate, set by the lender, can vary depending on factors like your credit score, the loan term, and market conditions.

Property Taxes: These taxes are levied by local governments to fund public services like schools, roads, and fire departments. While you may pay property taxes separately, many mortgage lenders include them in your monthly payment, creating an escrow account to ensure these taxes are paid on time.

Homeowners Insurance: This policy protects you against potential financial losses due to damage or theft to your property. Like property taxes, homeowners insurance is often bundled into your mortgage payment through an escrow account.

Private Mortgage Insurance (PMI): If your down payment is less than 20% of the purchase price, you'll likely have to pay PMI, a kind of insurance policy that protects the lender if you default on your loan. This adds to your monthly payment.

Navigating the Mortgage Maze: Fixed vs. Adjustable Rates

Mortgages come in different flavors, each with its own set of rules and financial implications. Two common types are fixed-rate and adjustable-rate mortgages.

Fixed-Rate Mortgages: In this scenario, your interest rate stays locked in for the entire duration of the loan. This provides predictability and peace of mind, allowing you to budget with confidence, knowing your monthly payment will remain consistent.

Adjustable-Rate Mortgages (ARMs): ARMs offer an initial lower interest rate, often making them tempting for borrowers. However, the interest rate fluctuates over time, typically adjusting periodically based on market benchmarks. This variability can lead to unpredictable monthly payments.

The Impact of Loan Term on Your Payments

The loan term, the length of time you have to repay your mortgage, is another crucial factor in determining your monthly payment. A longer term means lower monthly payments, but you'll end up paying more interest over the life of the loan. Conversely, a shorter term leads to higher payments but less interest paid overall.

The Power of Amortization: Understanding How Payments Work

Mortgage payments are not simply lump sums paid towards the principal. They are structured through a process called amortization, where each payment is allocated towards both the principal and interest.

Early Stages: At the beginning of your loan term, the majority of your payment goes towards interest, with a smaller portion allocated to the principal. You're effectively paying more for the privilege of borrowing the money.

Later Stages: As time goes on, the balance of your loan decreases, and more of your payment goes towards the principal. This leads to a gradual decline in the amount of interest you pay, eventually becoming a smaller portion of your total payment.

The Importance of a Realistic Budget

When you're dreaming of owning a home, it's easy to get caught up in the excitement and overlook the financial implications. A realistic budget is crucial to determine if homeownership is financially feasible and to avoid potential pitfalls.

Factor in More than the Mortgage Payment: Remember that the mortgage payment is just one piece of the homeownership puzzle. You'll also need to account for property taxes, homeowners' insurance, maintenance costs, utilities, and any homeowners' association fees.

Consider Your Lifestyle and Financial Goals: Evaluate your current financial situation, income, and expenses. Can you comfortably afford the added expenses of homeownership without compromising on your other financial goals, like retirement savings or travel?

Don't Forget the Unexpected: Life throws curveballs. Set aside a financial cushion for unexpected repairs or maintenance costs that might arise.

The Long-Term Financial Impact of Mortgage Payments

Mortgages are a long-term commitment, and their impact extends far beyond the monthly payment.

The "Dreaded" Interest: While initially a necessary cost of borrowing money, interest can amount to a substantial sum over the life of your loan—the more interest you pay, the less money you have available for other financial priorities.

The Equity Game: As you make your monthly mortgage payments, you build equity in your home. Equity is the difference between the market value of your home and the outstanding mortgage balance. Over time, your equity grows, giving you a financial stake in your property.

The Tax Advantages: Interest payments on a mortgage are typically deductible on your federal income taxes, providing potential tax savings. However, the deductibility is subject to income limits and other rules.

Navigating the Mortgage Process: The Power of Preparation

The mortgage process can be overwhelming, but it's essential to be informed and proactive to navigate the complexities effectively.

Shop Around for the Best Rates: Don't settle for the first mortgage offer you receive. Compare rates and terms from multiple lenders to secure the best deal.

Improve Your Credit Score: A higher credit score translates to lower interest rates, saving you money in the long run.

Understand the Loan Terms: Read the loan agreement carefully, paying particular attention to the interest rate, loan term, and any hidden fees.

Consult a Financial Advisor: Seek expert guidance from a trusted financial advisor to help you understand the financial implications of a mortgage and make informed decisions.

The Bottom Line:

The mortgage is a critical component of homeownership, influencing your long-term financial well-being. Understanding its mechanics, carefully budgeting, and seeking expert advice are vital steps in making informed decisions. Remember, homeownership is a journey, and like any journey, it's essential to be well-prepared and equipped to navigate the challenges and rewards along the way.

Property taxes are a significant hidden cost of homeownership that often catches new homeowners by surprise. They are essentially a tax levied by local governments on the assessed value of your property. While the exact rates vary widely depending on your location, they can represent a substantial chunk of your annual budget.

Imagine yourself, fresh out of college, finally stepping into your first home. The thrill of owning a piece of the American dream is palpable. You meticulously budget for your mortgage payments, knowing that they will be the lion's share of your expenses. You also factor in homeowners insurance, which, while not insignificant, feels manageable. But then comes the annual property tax bill, hitting you like a bolt out of the blue. You realize that you haven't budgeted for it, and now you are scrambling to make ends meet. This is a scenario that plays out all too often for unsuspecting homeowners.

The burden of property taxes can vary significantly depending on your state and local municipality. Some areas, particularly in states like New Jersey, Illinois, and Texas, have notoriously high property tax rates. Others, like Delaware, Nevada, and Hawaii, boast much lower rates. This stark disparity can make a significant difference in your overall housing costs, and it's something you need to consider carefully when evaluating potential homes.

For instance, let's compare two cities with different property tax rates. You might find a charming bungalow in a suburban neighborhood in a state like Nevada with a property tax rate of around 1%. If the assessed value of the home is $300,000, your annual property tax bill would be $3,000. Now, let's consider a similar bungalow in a suburban neighborhood in New Jersey, where the property tax rate might be as high as 2.5%. The same $300,000 assessed value would translate to an annual property tax bill of $7,500, more than double the cost in Nevada. This example highlights the vast differences in property tax rates across the country and how they can significantly impact your budget.

Beyond the differences between states, property taxes can also vary within a single city. Different neighborhoods within a city might have different tax rates, reflecting factors like the quality of local schools, the presence of public amenities, and the overall value of properties in the area. This means that even if you are set on a particular city, it's crucial to research the property tax rates in different neighborhoods to find the best value for your money.

Furthermore, property tax rates are not static. Local governments regularly adjust them based on factors such as inflation, budget needs, and property value assessments. This means that your property tax bill can increase year after year, even if your property value remains the same. While the exact amount of the increase might be relatively small, it's important to consider the potential for long-term growth in your property tax burden.

But the true burden of property taxes goes beyond the actual dollar amount. They have a profound impact on your overall financial well-being, influencing your purchasing power and investment decisions. Imagine you are saving for retirement, hoping to build a nest egg that will allow you to enjoy your golden years. If you are also paying high property taxes, it can significantly eat into your savings potential, forcing you to postpone your retirement goals. This is a common scenario for homeowners in high-tax areas, where the burden of property taxes can feel like an invisible tax on their financial freedom.

Moreover, property taxes can create a barrier to homeownership for many individuals. For young professionals just starting their careers, the prospect of large down payments, mortgage payments, and property taxes can feel overwhelming. It can make homeownership seem like a distant dream, forcing them to remain in rental apartments or delaying their entry into the housing market. This situation can be particularly challenging in areas with high property values and high property tax rates, creating a vicious cycle that makes it increasingly difficult for younger generations to enter the market.

It is crucial to understand the nuances of property taxes and their potential impact on your budget. While homeownership can be a valuable investment, it comes with its own set of financial responsibilities, and property taxes are one of the most significant. Before you leap into homeownership, it's essential to research the property tax rates in your target area, carefully consider their impact on your finances, and develop a realistic budget that accounts for these costs.

As you navigate the complexities of homeownership, it's important to remember that there are alternatives. Renting can offer significant financial benefits, such as increased liquidity and freedom from the burdens of property taxes and maintenance costs. For some individuals, renting might be a more financially sound decision, allowing them to focus on other financial goals, such as investing for retirement or pursuing their passions.

The decision of whether to rent or buy is a highly personal one, with no single "right" answer. But by understanding the hidden costs of homeownership, including the burden of property taxes, you can make an informed decision that aligns with your financial goals and lifestyle preferences. Remember, owning a home is not always the best financial decision, and there are compelling reasons to explore other options that might be more suitable for your situation.

Beyond the mortgage payments and property taxes, the true cost of homeownership lies in the ongoing expenses that can easily slip through the cracks. Imagine your home as a living, breathing entity, constantly demanding attention and resources.

Just like a pet, it requires regular care and feeding, and sometimes, even unexpected medical bills!

Let's dive into the world of home insurance and maintenance, two unsung heroes of homeownership that can significantly impact your financial well-being.

Home Insurance: A Safety Net with a Price Tag

Imagine your dream home, meticulously decorated and filled with cherished memories. Now imagine a fire, a flood, or a break-in ripping through it all, leaving behind devastation and financial ruin. Home insurance acts as a safety net, providing financial protection in the face of such unforeseen calamities. But just like any insurance, it comes with a price tag.

Understanding the Cost:

Home insurance premiums are determined by a variety of factors, including:

Location: Homes located in areas prone to natural disasters like earthquakes, floods, or hurricanes typically command higher premiums.

Property Value: The higher the value of your home, the more expensive it is to insure.

Coverage Levels: The amount of coverage you choose directly impacts your premium. A higher coverage limit means more protection but also higher costs.

Deductibles: The amount you're willing to pay out of pocket before insurance kicks in affects your premium. Higher deductibles translate to lower premiums and vice versa.

Home Features: Unique features like swimming pools, detached garages, or expensive landscaping can influence premiums.

Your Risk Profile: Your credit score and past claims history also play a role in determining your rates.

Beyond the Basic Coverage:

Basic home insurance typically covers damage caused by fire, theft, and natural disasters, but additional coverage options are available:

Flood Insurance: Often required in flood-prone areas, this coverage protects against water damage from flooding.

Earthquake Insurance: If you live in an earthquake-prone region, this is essential for safeguarding your home.

Liability Coverage: This covers you if someone gets injured on your property.

Personal Property Coverage: This covers your belongings inside the house, including furniture, electronics, and clothing.

Minimizing Costs:

While you can't control some factors like your location, you can take steps to lower your premiums:

Shop Around: Don't settle for the first quote you get. Compare rates from different insurers to find the best deal.

Increase Deductibles: If you're comfortable with a higher out-of-pocket expense in case of a claim, raising your deductible can save you money on premiums.

Improve Home Security: Adding security systems,

installing smoke detectors, and keeping your property well-lit can lower premiums by reducing your risk profile.

Bundle Policies: Combining your home insurance with other policies, like car insurance, can often lead to discounts.

Maintenance: The Silent Hero of Homeownership

Just like a car needs regular oil changes and tire rotations, your home requires ongoing maintenance to stay in top shape. These maintenance tasks may seem small and insignificant, but neglecting them can lead to costly repairs down the road.

Essential Maintenance Tasks:

Roof Inspection: Regular inspections ensure your roof is in good condition and can withstand the elements.

HVAC System Maintenance: Regular servicing ensures your heating and cooling system functions efficiently, saving you money on energy bills and preventing costly breakdowns.

Plumbing Checkups: Prevent plumbing problems like leaks and clogs by having your pipes and fixtures inspected regularly.

Exterior Maintenance: Regular cleaning and painting help maintain your home's curb appeal and protect it from weather damage.

Gutter Cleaning: Clean gutters prevent water damage and foundation problems.

Appliance Maintenance: Regularly check and maintain appliances to prevent unexpected breakdowns.

The Cost of Neglect:

Neglecting essential maintenance can lead to:

Increased Repair Costs: Small issues left unaddressed can escalate into larger problems, resulting in more expensive repairs.

Reduced Home Value: A poorly maintained home will have a lower resale value compared to a well-maintained one.

Safety Hazards: Faulty appliances, leaky pipes, or structural problems can create safety risks for you and your family.

The Importance of Regular Maintenance:

Regular maintenance, while requiring an investment, pays dividends in the long run by:

Extending the Life of Your Home: Proper care can significantly increase the lifespan of your house, saving you money on replacements and renovations.

Preventing Costly Repairs: Early detection and addressing minor issues can prevent them from becoming major problems.

Increasing Energy Efficiency: Maintaining appliances and HVAC systems can save you money on utility bills.

Enhancing Resale Value: A well-maintained home is more attractive to potential buyers, leading to a higher sale price.

DIY vs. Professional Services:

Many basic maintenance tasks can be tackled with DIY skills, while others are best left to professionals.

DIY Options:

Basic Cleaning: You can handle regular cleaning of windows, gutters, and surfaces yourself.

Simple Repairs: Minor repairs like fixing leaky faucets, replacing light bulbs, or painting can be done by homeowners with basic skills.

Landscaping: Taking care of your lawn and garden can be a satisfying DIY project. Professional Services:

Complex Repairs: Major repairs like roofing, plumbing, electrical, or HVAC work should be entrusted to licensed professionals for safety and quality assurance.

Structural Issues: If you notice cracks in your foundation or walls, it's crucial to call a structural engineer or a qualified contractor for assessment and repairs.

Specialized Maintenance: Tasks like chimney inspections, well water testing, or pest control require specialized expertise and should be handled by qualified professionals.

Creating a Maintenance Budget:

To ensure you have the funds readily available for ongoing maintenance, it's essential to create a maintenance budget:

Estimate Annual Costs: Research average costs for typical maintenance tasks in your area and create a realistic estimate for your home.

Set Aside Funds: Regularly set aside a portion of your monthly budget to cover these costs.

Establish a Maintenance Schedule: Develop a schedule for regular inspections and maintenance tasks, ensuring they are addressed promptly.

The Value of Routine and Proactive Action

Home insurance and maintenance may seem like hidden costs that chip away at your budget. However, they are essential investments that safeguard your home, your financial well-being, and your peace of mind. By understanding these costs and adopting a proactive approach, you can manage them effectively and ensure your home remains a haven for years to come.

Imagine you've just bought your dream home. You're excited, envisioning family gatherings, cozy evenings by the fireplace, and the joy of creating memories within those walls. However, lurking beneath the surface of that excitement is a reality that many homeowners often fail to grasp fully: the potential for depreciation.

Home values, unlike many investments, aren't guaranteed to climb steadily upwards. They can, in fact, decline. This depreciation can stem from various factors, including market fluctuations, economic downturns, changes in local demographics, or even the simple wear and tear that comes with time.

Think of your home as a tangible asset, like a car. Just as a car loses value the moment you drive it off the lot, your home will likely depreciate over time. It's a sobering thought, but one that's essential to consider when weighing the pros and cons of homeownership.

The concept of "equity" is closely linked to depreciation. Equity represents the portion of your home's value that you actually own. As you make mortgage payments, your equity gradually increases, as the amount you owe decreases. But here's the catch: if your home's value drops, your equity can shrink, too.

Let's break down the impact of depreciation with a real-life example. Suppose you bought a home for $300,000 with a $100,000 down payment. You start with $200,000 in mortgage debt and $100,000 in equity. Five years later, you've diligently made your mortgage payments and reduced your debt to $150,000, meaning your equity has risen to $150,000. Sounds fantastic, right?

But what if, during those five years, the housing market in your area experiences a downturn? Your home's market value might plummet to $250,000. Now, even though your equity has grown based on your mortgage payments, your actual equity is only

$50,000. This means your home is worth less than you originally paid for it, despite your ongoing investment.

The scenario above illustrates a crucial point: while mortgage payments contribute to building equity, the value of your home, and therefore your equity, is subject to market forces beyond your control.

Now, let's delve into some of the key factors that can cause depreciation:

1. **Market Fluctuations:**

The housing market isn't always a smooth upward climb. It experiences cyclical swings influenced by factors like interest rates, economic growth, and consumer confidence. When interest rates rise, borrowing becomes more expensive, leading to decreased demand for homes and potentially pushing prices down.

Similarly, economic downturns can have a ripple effect on the housing market. Job losses, reduced consumer spending, and decreased economic activity can all contribute to a decline in housing values.

2. **Local Economic Factors:**

While national economic trends play a role, local economic factors can also influence housing prices. Consider the example of a town heavily reliant on a specific industry, like manufacturing. If that industry experiences a downturn or relocation, it can significantly impact the local economy and, consequently, housing values.

3. **Demographic Shifts:**

Changes in population demographics, such as aging populations or an influx of new residents, can affect demand for specific types of housing. For instance, if a neighborhood experiences an influx of families, the demand for larger homes with good school districts might increase, driving up prices. Conversely, if an area experiences an exodus of young professionals, the demand for smaller, more affordable homes might decrease, leading to depreciation.

4. **Property Condition and Maintenance:**

While a well-maintained home can hold its value, neglect and lack of upkeep can contribute to depreciation. A home with peeling paint, a leaky roof, or a neglected yard may be less desirable to potential buyers, resulting in a lower market value.

5. **Neighborhood Deterioration:**

The surrounding neighborhood also plays a role in home values. If a once-thriving area experiences a decline in property values, crime rates, or overall neighborhood maintenance, your home's value might be affected, even if you maintain your property meticulously.

6. **Natural Disasters and Environmental Issues:**

Natural disasters such as hurricanes, earthquakes, or floods can significantly impact home values. Even if your home remains intact, the perception of risk in the area can lead to depreciation. Similarly, environmental issues, such as pollution or soil contamination, can negatively affect housing prices.

7. **Changes in Local Regulations and Zoning:**

New zoning laws, building codes, or tax regulations can influence the desirability of a property. For instance, if an area is rezoned to allow for increased density, the value of existing single-family homes might decrease due to increased competition or potential changes in the neighborhood's character.

8. **Interest Rates and Loan Terms:**

Interest rates are a key factor influencing the cost of borrowing money for a mortgage. When interest rates are high, mortgage payments are also higher, leading to reduced affordability and potentially slowing down home sales, affecting prices.

Similarly, the terms of your mortgage, such as the length of the loan and the interest rate type, can affect your overall borrowing costs and the amount you owe, impacting your equity.

9. **Availability of Housing Inventory:**

In a housing market with limited inventory, sellers often have an advantage, as buyers face fewer options and are willing to pay higher prices. Conversely, when inventory is abundant, buyers have more choices, potentially driving down prices as sellers compete for attention.

10. **Market Sentiment and Speculation:**

Market sentiment, or the overall mood and expectations of buyers and sellers, can also influence housing values. During periods of uncertainty or economic turmoil, buyers may become hesitant, causing prices to stagnate or even decline. Conversely, a strong economy and positive market sentiment can lead to increased demand and higher prices. Speculation in the housing market can also create bubbles, where prices rise artificially, eventually leading to a correction and a drop in values.

It's crucial to understand that depreciation is a reality for most tangible assets, and homes are no exception. While you can't control all of the factors that influence home values, being aware of these potential pitfalls is essential for making informed decisions about homeownership.

Understanding the Implications of Depreciation

Now that we've explored the causes of depreciation, let's delve into its implications for homeowners.

1. **Reduced Equity:**

As mentioned earlier, depreciation can erode your equity—the portion of your home's value that you own. This reduced equity can have significant financial consequences if you decide to sell your home, as you'll receive less money than you initially invested. Furthermore, if you need to access equity through a home equity loan or line of credit, a lower home value can limit the amount you can borrow.

2. **Difficulty Selling or Refinancing:**

If your home's value has depreciated, it can be challenging to sell it at a profitable price. Potential buyers might be hesitant to pay the asking price if they perceive the home's value to be lower than your asking price, especially in a slow market. Similarly, refinancing your mortgage might be difficult if your home's value has decreased, as lenders typically assess loan approvals based on the appraised value of the property.

3. **Impact on Financial Planning:**

Depreciation can disrupt your long-term financial plans. If you're planning to use your home's equity for retirement, downsizing, or other financial goals, a decline in value can derail those plans. It's essential to factor in the potential for depreciation when developing your financial strategy, especially if you're relying on your home's value as a source of future wealth.

4. **Potential for Negative Equity:**

In a worst-case scenario, depreciation could lead to negative equity, where your home's value falls below the amount you owe on your mortgage. This situation can be stressful and financially challenging. If you're facing negative equity, you might be unable to sell your home without incurring a financial loss, as the proceeds from the sale wouldn't be enough to cover your mortgage debt.

5. **Psychological Impact:**

The realization that your home's value is declining can have a psychological impact. It can create feelings of anxiety, frustration, and even regret. However, it's important to remember that depreciation is often a temporary phenomenon, and markets tend to cycle through periods of growth and decline. Focusing on the long-term picture and understanding the factors influencing your local market can help you manage these emotions.

Managing the Risks of Depreciation

While you can't eliminate the risk of depreciation, you can take steps to mitigate its impact.

1. **Thorough Research and Due Diligence:**

Before purchasing a home, conduct thorough research on the local housing market. Analyze historical trends, economic conditions, and demographic shifts in the area. Consider factors such as job growth, school quality, crime rates, and infrastructure development. Don't just rely on real estate agents' opinions; conduct your investigation and compare data from different sources.

2. **Prudent Location Selection:**

Choose a location that has a strong economic foundation and is resistant to market downturns. Look for areas with diverse industries, a healthy job market, and a good track record of stable home values. Avoid areas that are highly speculative or dependent on a single industry.

3. **Consider Loan Terms:**

Carefully consider your mortgage terms, including interest rate, loan term, and amortization schedule. A shorter loan term, like a 15-year mortgage, can help you build equity faster and reduce your overall interest payments, but it comes with higher monthly payments. Conversely, a longer loan term, like a 30-year mortgage, offers lower monthly payments but allows for more interest to accrue over time.

4. **Invest in Maintenance and Upgrades:**

Regularly maintain your home to prevent deterioration and keep its value intact. Address any repairs or upgrades promptly, as neglecting maintenance can lead to larger, more expensive problems down the line. Make smart investments in upgrades that increase the value of your home, such as kitchen and bathroom renovations, energy-efficient appliances, or landscaping improvements.

5. **Diversify Your Investments:**

Don't rely solely on your home as your sole investment. Diversify your portfolio by investing in other assets, such as stocks, bonds, and real estate investment trusts (REITs). This diversification can help you weather potential downturns in the housing market and create a more resilient financial foundation.

6. **Develop a Realistic Financial Plan:**

Create a financial plan that accounts for the potential for depreciation and other unforeseen circumstances. Include emergency savings, a budget for home maintenance, and a plan for managing debt. Consider the possibility that you might need to sell your home before it fully appreciates, and factor in any potential financial implications.

7. **Stay Informed and Adapt:**

Stay up-to-date on local and national economic trends, as well as changes in the housing market. Monitor interest rates, economic data, and property values in your area. Be prepared to adapt your financial plan and your homeownership strategy based on market conditions.

8. **Embrace the Long-Term Perspective:**

Homeownership is often a long-term investment. Don't make decisions solely based on short-term market fluctuations. Focus on the long-term potential of your home, its ability to provide a stable place to live, and its potential to generate equity over time.

9. **Seek Professional Advice:**

Consult with a financial advisor or real estate professional to get expert guidance on homeownership. They can help you navigate the complexities of the housing market, assess your financial situation, and develop a customized strategy for managing the risks of depreciation.

10. **Don't Panic:**

Remember that depreciation is a normal part of the real estate cycle. If your home's value declines, don't panic. Stay calm, assess the situation, and take steps to mitigate the impact. Focus on your long-term goals and keep a positive outlook.

Conclusion

The potential for depreciation is a hidden cost of homeownership that many people overlook. While homeownership offers many benefits, it's crucial to acknowledge the risk of depreciation and take steps to manage it effectively. By understanding the factors that can cause depreciation, developing a realistic financial plan, and making informed decisions, you can minimize the impact of depreciation and enjoy the benefits of homeownership with greater financial security.

Remember, homeownership is a marathon, not a sprint. It requires patience, planning, and a long-term perspective. By embracing these principles and approaching homeownership with a realistic mindset, you can navigate the ups and downs of the housing market and achieve your long-term financial goals.

The idea that a home is a foolproof investment is deeply ingrained in our cultural narrative. We've been told, time and time again, that owning a home is the key to building wealth, achieving financial security, and even securing a brighter future. This narrative is so pervasive that it can feel like a truth beyond question. But what if this widely accepted belief is not entirely accurate? What if, in reality, homeownership is not always the best financial decision, and the potential pitfalls are often brushed aside in favor of a romanticized vision?

Let's peel back the layers of this ingrained belief and confront some uncomfortable truths. The reality is that owning a home comes with a complex web of hidden costs, financial burdens, and unforeseen circumstances that can easily derail your financial plans.

First, consider the ongoing cost of mortgage payments. These payments are more than just the principal and interest—they also include property taxes, homeowners insurance, and private mortgage insurance (PMI) if your down payment was less than 20%. These monthly expenses can stretch your budget thin, especially in high-cost areas where property taxes and insurance premiums can be substantial.

Beyond the mortgage, there's the constant need for repairs and maintenance. Your home is not a static entity; it's a living, breathing structure that requires ongoing attention. From minor repairs like leaky faucets and clogged drains to major renovations like roof replacements and HVAC upgrades, these unexpected expenses can quickly drain your savings and add significant stress to your financial well-being. Another crucial aspect to consider is property taxes. Property taxes are calculated based on the assessed value of your property and can vary widely from state to state and even from county to county. The burden of property taxes can be a significant financial drain, especially in areas with high property valuations. While property taxes are generally used to fund local schools and other public services, they still contribute to the overall cost of homeownership.

Even if you manage to navigate the mortgage payments, property taxes, and maintenance costs, you still face the risk of market fluctuations and depreciation. The housing market is not a linear upward trajectory; it's cyclical, subject to booms and busts, economic downturns, and various other factors. If you happen to buy a home at the peak of a market bubble, you could find yourself stuck with a property that has lost significant value, putting your equity and potential for future profit at risk. It's important to remember that owning a home is not a passive investment; it requires constant attention and financial commitment. While you may be able to generate some passive income from renting out a room or a part of your property; this often comes with its own set of challenges, such as finding reliable tenants, managing property upkeep, and dealing with tenant issues.

The reality is that homeownership is not a surefire path to wealth accumulation. While the potential for appreciation and equity building exists, it is not guaranteed. The housing market is subject to numerous variables, including economic conditions, interest rates, local market trends, and even natural disasters, all of which can significantly impact the value of your investment.

Moreover, homeownership can often lock you into a location, making it difficult to relocate for better job opportunities or lifestyle changes. Moving can be a costly and time-consuming process, especially if you need to sell a property. This can be a major drawback for those in industries that require frequent relocation or for those who simply crave the flexibility to explore new horizons.

In a world where job security and financial stability are constantly being redefined, the traditional idea of homeownership as the ultimate financial goal might be outdated. The flexibility and freedom offered by renting can be invaluable, especially for young professionals, individuals with nomadic lifestyles, or those who value the ability to adapt to changing circumstances.

Renting offers a more fluid and less financially demanding way to live. You have the flexibility to move to a new city, a different neighborhood, or even a new country without the hassle of selling a property. This freedom allows you to pursue career opportunities, follow your passions, and embrace a more adventurous and adaptable lifestyle.

Furthermore, renting can provide a significant financial advantage. By avoiding the large down payment required for homeownership, you can free up your savings and investments to pursue other financial goals, such as paying down debt, building an emergency fund, or investing in your retirement.

The choice between renting and owning is ultimately a personal one, and there's no one-size-fits-all answer. It's crucial to weigh the pros and cons of both options, considering your individual circumstances, financial goals, and lifestyle preferences. This book is intended to provide you with a broader perspective, challenging the conventional wisdom and presenting a more nuanced view of homeownership. It's not about advocating for one choice over another; it's about empowering you with the information and insights to make the most informed decision for your unique situation.

By embracing a critical and analytical approach to this crucial financial decision, you can break free from the societal pressures and expectations that often cloud our judgment. You can make choices that truly align with your financial goals, lifestyle aspirations, and overall well-being.

THE CHALLENGES OF RENTING

2

THE CASE FOR RENTING

Imagine this: you're in your early 20s, fresh out of college, and you've landed your dream job in a bustling city. You're excited about the possibilities, but the prospect of buying a home feels overwhelming. The thought of a hefty down payment, soaring mortgage rates, and the constant pressure of maintaining a property seems daunting. You're still figuring out your career path, and the idea of being tied down to a location feels restrictive.

Renting, on the other hand, offers a breath of fresh air. It allows you to be flexible, embrace new opportunities, and enjoy the freedom to move without the burden of selling a house. Renting is your passport to a life filled with adventure and discovery, allowing you to explore different neighborhoods, cities, and even countries without the constraints of property ownership.

Think of it this way: renting gives you the flexibility to chase your dreams, whether it's trying out a new city for a year, pursuing a graduate degree in a different state, or simply switching jobs in a new neighborhood. You're not tied down to a fixed location, giving you the freedom to explore the world and adapt to life's unpredictable turns.

But the benefits of renting go beyond just flexibility. It also frees you from the financial burden of homeownership, allowing you to allocate your resources more strategically. You can use the money you would have spent on a down payment, mortgage payments, property taxes, and maintenance costs to invest in your future, build a robust emergency fund, or indulge in experiences that enrich your life.

Consider a young professional who chooses to rent in a vibrant city center. Instead of spending their hard-earned money on mortgages and property maintenance, they can invest in their professional development, take exciting vacations, or build healthy savings accounts for the future. They can also leverage the lower monthly rent payments to live in a trendy neighborhood, close to cultural hotspots, and enjoy a vibrant social scene.

Now, let's shift our focus to a different scenario: a couple in their 50s, approaching retirement. They've spent years building a career and raising a family, but they're starting to think about their future. They've accumulated a sizable amount of equity in their home, but they're realizing that the upkeep is becoming more demanding and expensive. They're also dreaming of exploring new horizons, traveling the world, and enjoying a relaxing lifestyle in a warmer climate.

Renting provides an attractive alternative for this couple. They can sell their home, freeing up a significant amount of capital. This money can be used to fund their retirement years, invest in travel experiences, or move to a more affordable location where they can enjoy their golden years in comfort. They can rent a spacious apartment in a charming coastal town, freeing themselves from the responsibility of maintaining a large home and embracing a more carefree lifestyle.

Renting doesn't necessarily mean sacrificing the comforts of home ownership. You can still find well-maintained, modern apartments that offer all the amenities you need, including spacious layouts, in-unit laundry, and even access to community amenities like swimming pools and fitness centers. You can enjoy a similar level of comfort and convenience without the burden of ownership.

Imagine a retiree who opts to rent a cozy apartment in a sunny Mediterranean town. Instead of worrying about roof repairs and yard maintenance, they can focus on their passions, spending their days exploring local markets, enjoying leisurely strolls by the sea, and spending quality time with their loved ones. They can also connect with a vibrant community of fellow retirees, expanding their social circle and enriching their lives.

In conclusion, renting isn't just about saving money or avoiding the hassles of homeownership. It's about embracing a life filled with flexibility, freedom, and opportunities. It's about saying yes to new experiences, chasing your dreams, and living life on your own terms. Renting is a powerful tool that empowers you to create a life that aligns with your values and aspirations. It's a choice that allows you to embrace change, explore the world, and make the most of every stage in your life's journey.

Imagine a world where you are not bound to a single place, where your financial future isn't tethered to the fluctuating value of a brick-and-mortar structure. This is the world of renting, where flexibility, freedom, and financial security intertwine.

While many believe homeownership is the holy grail of financial success, we're here to challenge that notion. We'll delve into the hidden costs and potential downsides of homeownership, revealing the often-overlooked burdens that come with owning a home. We'll explore the financial implications of renting, unveiling the hidden advantages and potential for savings.

Renting often gets a bad rap, portrayed as a "throwing money away" scenario. But, what if we told you that renting can actually be a strategic financial move, liberating you from the shackles of a fixed mortgage and allowing you to build a more secure financial future?

Here's why:

Financial Liquidity and Savings Potential

Picture this: You're in your early 20s, starting your career. You're presented with two paths: buy a house or rent. The conventional wisdom whispers, "Buy, buy, buy!" But, let's examine this from a different perspective.

Buying a house requires a significant down payment, often tied to a hefty mortgage. This means you're tying up a substantial portion of your savings and potentially limiting your ability to invest in other ventures, such as your education, starting a business, or building an emergency fund.

On the other hand, renting allows you to maintain financial liquidity. You can use your savings to invest in the stock market, explore business opportunities, or simply build a comfortable safety net.

Let's break down the financial benefits of renting:

1. **Lower upfront costs:** The cost of buying a house is significant. You need to put down a hefty down payment, often 20% of the purchase price, and cover closing costs, which can easily add up to thousands of dollars. Renting, on the other hand, usually requires a smaller security deposit and the first month's rent. This lower upfront cost allows you to allocate your money towards other financial goals.
2. **Predictable monthly expenses:** Rent payments are typically fixed, giving you a clearer picture of your monthly expenses. Homeownership, however, comes

with unexpected costs, like property taxes, insurance premiums, and repairs. These costs can fluctuate, creating a less predictable budget.

3. **Flexibility and relocation ease:** Renting offers the flexibility to move when your life circumstances change. If you get a new job in another city or simply want to explore different neighborhoods, renting makes it easier to transition. Homeownership, however, can tie you down to a location for longer, potentially hindering your career advancement or personal growth.
4. **Avoiding costly repairs and maintenance:** As a renter, you're typically not responsible for major repairs and maintenance. The landlord handles those expenses, which can be a significant financial burden for homeowners. You only pay for the repairs you cause, and your landlord is responsible for everything else.
5. **Opportunity to build a strong emergency fund:** Renting allows you to allocate a larger portion of your income towards savings. You can build a robust emergency fund to cover unexpected expenses like medical bills, job loss, or travel emergencies.

Real-World Examples:

Sarah, the aspiring entrepreneur: Sarah is a 27-year-old marketing professional who wants to start her own digital marketing agency. She's living in a trendy apartment in a bustling city center, strategically located near her potential clients and networking opportunities. She's chosen to rent, understanding that buying a house at this point would tie up significant funds, potentially hindering her business venture. Sarah invests her savings in her business, confident in her ability to relocate if needed.

David, the early retiree: David, 55, decided to retire early and move to a tropical island. He opted to rent a cozy beach-front apartment, freeing up his capital to explore different investment opportunities and fund his adventures.

Maria, the single mother: Maria is a single mom in her late 30s. She chooses to rent a spacious apartment in a family-friendly neighborhood near good schools. By renting, she can focus on her children's needs without the burden of homeownership responsibilities. She can easily move if her circumstances change, ensuring a safe and stable environment for her children.

More Than Just Money

Beyond the financial benefits, renting offers a sense of freedom that's often overlooked. It allows you to embrace a more minimalist lifestyle, freeing you from the stress and responsibilities that can accompany homeownership.

Imagine the freedom of packing up your belongings, hopping on a plane, and exploring a new city, country, or continent without the constraints of a mortgage or property taxes. Imagine the joy of traveling without the worry of leaving your home vacant or the fear of missing out on a lucrative opportunity because of a tied-down lifestyle.

A Matter of Perspective

Renting is not about being "stuck" or "settling." It's about taking control of your finances, embracing your freedom, and investing in your future. It's about understanding that a house doesn't define your worth, and that true wealth lies in financial flexibility, personal growth, and the ability to pursue your passions.

Remember, the key is to approach your housing choices strategically, considering your individual needs and financial goals. Renting can be a powerful tool to achieve financial security, explore new opportunities, and ultimately, live a life that aligns with your values.

So, challenge the traditional narrative, explore the world of renting, and discover a path to financial freedom that suits your own unique journey. You might just find that renting is the perfect stepping stone to a life filled with possibilities.

Imagine you're standing at a crossroads, one path leading to the traditional American dream of owning a home, the other to a world of renting, flexibility, and financial freedom. The allure of homeownership, with its promise of stability and equity, is undeniable. However, as we've explored, the hidden costs and complexities can quickly turn this dream into a financial burden. This is where the beauty of renting shines through, offering a path less traveled, yet often more liberating.

Renting allows you to embrace the freedom of choice. Unlike homeowners who are tethered to their property, renters can move at a moment's notice, chasing new opportunities, exploring different cities, or simply seeking a change of scenery. This flexibility is particularly valuable for young professionals whose careers may require frequent relocations, or for retirees who are eager to experience new adventures in their golden years.

Beyond the freedom of movement, renting presents significant financial benefits. You're shielded from the unpredictable fluctuations of the housing market, avoiding potential losses in equity or the stress of dealing with unexpected repairs. The absence of mortgage payments frees up a significant portion of your income, allowing you to invest in your future, travel the world, or pursue your passions.

Furthermore, renting grants you financial liquidity. This means that your money isn't tied up in a depreciating asset, allowing you to access your savings for important life events like starting a business, funding your children's education, or simply enjoying peace of mind knowing you have a safety net.

But the benefits of renting extend far beyond the financial realm. It fosters a sense of freedom and liberation, allowing you to live life on your own terms. Imagine being able to pack up and move to a vibrant city without the hassle of selling a house or the fear of losing your investment. This sense of freedom can be incredibly empowering, allowing you to pursue your dreams without the constraints of homeownership.

Let's explore some of the common pitfalls homeowners face that renters can avoid:

The Ever-Present Maintenance Burden: Homeownership comes with an ongoing commitment to maintenance and repairs. From leaky faucets to roof repairs, unexpected issues can arise at any time, often with hefty price tags attached. While some homeowners choose to tackle these tasks themselves, many find themselves relying on expensive contractors, adding to the financial burden. Renters, on the other hand, have the luxury of letting their landlords handle these headaches. They can simply report any maintenance issues and let the professionals take care of them.

The Unsteady Terrain of Home Value Fluctuations: Homeowners often dream of their property appreciating in value, but the reality is that the housing market can be unpredictable. Interest rate changes, economic downturns, and even local events can impact home values, leading to potential losses in equity. Renters, however, are not directly affected by these fluctuations. Their rent remains relatively stable, providing them with a predictable monthly expense.

The Constant Cycle of Property Taxes: Property taxes, a substantial expense for homeowners, can vary significantly depending on your location. They can rise unexpectedly, putting a strain on your budget. Renters are relieved of this burden as property taxes are typically factored into the landlord's overall expenses.

The Hidden Costs of Homeownership: While the initial purchase price of a home may seem like the biggest hurdle, the ongoing costs of homeownership can quickly add up. This includes not only mortgage payments, property taxes, and insurance but also the constant upkeep of a property, from landscaping to painting to appliance replacements. These expenses can often be overlooked when considering the affordability of homeownership. Renters, in contrast, have a more predictable and often lower overall cost of living.

The Trap of Home Improvement Projects: The allure of home improvement projects is strong, with promises of increased value and personal satisfaction. However, these projects can quickly spiral out of control, both in terms of time and money. Even simple tasks can become complex and expensive, leading to unforeseen expenses and frustrations. Renters, on the other hand, can enjoy their living space without the responsibility or financial strain of renovation projects.

The Emotional and Psychological Burden of Homeownership: Homeownership comes with a lot of emotional and psychological baggage. The pressure to maintain a pristine property, keep up with the latest trends, and constantly improve the home can take a toll on your mental well-being. Renters, however, have the freedom to decorate and personalize their space without the pressure of making long-term investments. They can simply focus on creating a comfortable and enjoyable living environment, freeing up their energy for other pursuits.

The Limitations of Homeownership in a Mobile World: In today's world, where careers and personal pursuits often demand flexibility and adaptability, homeownership can feel like a constraint. The prospect of selling a home, finding a new one, and relocating can be a daunting and expensive undertaking. Renters, on the other hand, enjoy the flexibility to move at a moment's notice, embracing new opportunities and experiences without the burden of a tied-down asset.

The Real Estate Market's Unpredictability: The housing market, like any market, is subject to fluctuations. Interest rates, economic conditions, and even local events can influence property values. What was a lucrative investment today might be a financial burden tomorrow. Renters, however, are shielded from these fluctuations, enjoying a predictable and stable monthly rent.

The Cost of Ownership Over Time: The hidden costs of homeownership extend far beyond the initial purchase price. Homeowners must constantly factor in property taxes, insurance, maintenance expenses, and potential repairs, all of which can add up significantly over time. This can create a financial burden that can impact other aspects of life, such as retirement savings or travel plans.

The Financial Benefits of Renters: The financial advantages of renting are undeniable. Without the burden of mortgage payments, renters have more disposable income, allowing them to invest in their future, pursue their passions, or simply enjoy a higher quality of life. This financial flexibility allows them to take advantage of opportunities without being tied down by a significant financial obligation.

The Emotional Freedom of Renters: Beyond the financial benefits, renting offers an emotional freedom that can be just as liberating. Renters are free from the pressure of maintaining a property, keeping up with home improvement projects, and dealing with the complexities of the housing market. They can focus on creating a comfortable and enjoyable living environment without the constant worry of potential losses or financial strain.

The Practicalities of Renting: Renting offers a practical and affordable solution for a variety of lifestyles and situations. For young professionals navigating the early stages of their careers, renting provides flexibility and financial freedom, allowing them to pursue their dreams without being weighed down by homeownership. For retirees, renting provides an opportunity to downsize, reduce their expenses, and enjoy their golden years without the burden of a large mortgage. For families, renting offers the flexibility to choose neighborhoods with good schools, community resources, and affordable housing options without the financial strain of homeownership.

The Choice is Yours: Ultimately, the decision between renting and buying is a personal one. It depends on your individual circumstances, financial goals, and lifestyle preferences. However, by understanding the benefits and drawbacks of each option, you can make an informed decision that aligns with your vision for the future.

Embrace the Journey: Whether you choose the path of homeownership or the freedom of renting, remember that your home is not just a roof over your head. It's a reflection of your values, your aspirations, and your journey through life. Choose wisely, and let your home be a source of joy, comfort, and inspiration.

The allure of owning a home is undeniable. It's a symbol of stability, a tangible investment, and a place to build memories. But what if the traditional path to homeownership isn't the right fit for everyone? What if renting offers a more flexible and financially savvy approach to living?

This is where the power of renting shines. While homeownership comes with the weight of responsibility, renting allows you to embrace a life of flexibility and financial freedom. Imagine the ability to relocate at a moment's notice, without the burden of selling a property. Imagine having the flexibility to move to a new city for a job opportunity or simply to explore a different lifestyle. Renting offers a liberating perspective, letting you prioritize experiences and financial goals over the constraints of property ownership.

Let's dive into the heart of this chapter: exploring the world of renting, particularly in the context of bustling city centers versus the tranquil suburbs.

Renting in the Urban Jungle

For many young professionals, the allure of city life is irresistible. The vibrant energy, diverse cultures, and endless opportunities create a magnetic pull. Renting in a major city offers a front-row seat to the city's pulse, allowing you to experience its vibrant social scene, explore culinary delights, and immerse yourself in artistic expression.

However, with this urban lifestyle comes a unique set of considerations.

One of the biggest attractions is the proximity to work opportunities. Imagine walking to your office, enjoying a quick lunch break at a trendy café, and being surrounded by a network of professionals. The convenience and efficiency of urban living are undeniable, particularly for those in high-demand fields. The ability to connect with potential employers and expand your professional network can significantly boost your career trajectory.

Another key advantage is the abundance of public transportation. City dwellers often rely on buses, subways, or trains, reducing reliance on personal vehicles and saving on car payments, insurance, and parking fees. This not only saves money but also contributes to a more eco-conscious lifestyle, reducing one's carbon footprint.

However, renting in major cities often comes with a higher cost of living. The rent itself is typically higher than in suburban areas, and the convenience of city living translates into higher costs for dining out, entertainment, and even groceries. It's crucial to carefully consider your budget and ensure that your income aligns with the expenses associated with urban living.

Suburban Oasis: A Different Perspective

For families seeking a more spacious and tranquil environment, the suburbs offer a compelling alternative. Picture spacious homes with yards where children can play, quiet neighborhoods where the pace of life is slower, and a sense of community that fosters strong bonds between residents.

The suburbs often provide a more affordable option for renting, with lower rent prices and a greater variety of housing choices, from cozy apartments to single-family homes with yards. This affordability can significantly impact your financial well-being, leaving you with more disposable income for family activities, vacations, or even savings.

Suburban areas often boast excellent public schools, providing a solid foundation for your children's education. Many neighborhoods also feature parks, recreational facilities, and community centers, fostering a sense of community and offering opportunities for social interaction.

However, life in the suburbs comes with its own set of tradeoffs. The commute to work can be significantly longer, requiring more time and expense on transportation. Access to cultural attractions, restaurants, and entertainment options may be limited compared to the abundance found in urban centers.

The Perfect Fit: Finding the Balance

Ultimately, the choice between renting in a major city or the suburbs comes down to individual preferences and priorities. Consider your lifestyle, career aspirations, and family needs to determine which environment aligns best with your goals.

For young professionals seeking career advancement and a vibrant social scene, the excitement and opportunities of city life may be irresistible. For families prioritizing affordability, space, and a strong community, the suburbs offer a compelling alternative.

The Art of Renting: Beyond the Finances

While financial factors are undoubtedly crucial, it's essential to remember that renting is about more than just the bottom line. It's about embracing a life of flexibility, freedom, and the opportunity to discover new experiences.

Renting allows you to explore different neighborhoods, try out different lifestyles, and make choices that align with your evolving priorities. It's an opportunity to break free from the constraints of homeownership and embrace the adventure of living in the moment.

As you weigh the pros and cons of renting versus buying, consider the emotional and psychological benefits that renting offers. It allows you to live without the weight of mortgage payments, property taxes, and the constant stress of maintaining a home. You can focus on personal growth, building relationships, and pursuing your passions, knowing that you have the flexibility to move whenever you desire.

The beauty of renting lies in its ability to empower you to live a life on your own terms, free from the financial and emotional burdens of homeownership. It's a path that invites exploration, encourages adaptability, and opens the door to a world of possibilities.

Imagine yourself waking up on a Saturday morning, not to the sound of a lawnmower or the smell of freshly cut grass, but to the gentle hum of a nearby cafe. You step outside, and instead of tending to your own garden, you walk a few blocks to a farmers market, indulging in a leisurely brunch and soaking in the vibrant energy of your neighborhood. This isn't a scene from a fantasy novel; it's the everyday reality of a renter, embracing the freedom and flexibility that comes with choosing not to own a home.

For many, owning a home is a symbol of achievement, a milestone representing stability and success. Yet, this ingrained belief often overshadows the often-overlooked downsides of homeownership, from the financial burden of mortgage payments and property taxes to the unexpected costs of maintenance and repairs. The pressure to buy, fueled by societal expectations and the illusion of home as a guaranteed investment, can overshadow the genuine joy of living life on your own terms.

Renting, on the other hand, offers a different perspective. It's a choice that allows you to prioritize experiences over possessions, adventure over stability, and personal growth over financial constraints. It's a conscious decision to embrace the freedom to move, to change, and to adapt to life's ever-evolving circumstances.

Let's delve deeper into the psychological liberation that comes with renting. By freeing yourself from the weight of homeownership, you unlock a unique sense of mental and emotional freedom.

1. **Unburdening Yourself from the Financial and Time Commitments of Homeownership:**

Imagine this scenario: You've just received a job offer in a new city, one that promises career advancement and exciting new experiences. But there's a catch—you own a house. The thought of selling your home, dealing with real estate agents, and navigating the complexities of the housing market is daunting. The financial burden of carrying a mortgage, along with the potential for market fluctuations, weighs heavily on your mind. The dream of relocating feels more like a logistical nightmare.

As a renter, this situation takes on a completely different outlook. With a simple notice, you can move, embrace the opportunity, and embark on a new chapter in your life. Your monthly rent, often a fraction of your mortgage payment, allows you to maintain a sense of financial flexibility and stability, even amidst a major life change. This freedom extends beyond just relocation. It allows you to prioritize experiences over material possessions. Instead of sinking a large portion of your income into homeownership, you can explore the world, invest in your passions, or save for your future with greater ease.

2. **Living in the Present and Embracing Flexibility:**

Homeownership often comes with a sense of responsibility and commitment. It's a commitment to a specific location, a specific lifestyle, and a specific set of financial obligations. While this can be fulfilling for some, it can also feel limiting for others. It can create a sense of being tied down, of being anchored to a particular place, even if you're yearning for something more.

Renting, in contrast, embraces the fluidity of life. It allows you to experience different neighborhoods, try out different lifestyles, and adapt to your ever-changing needs.

This flexibility is a powerful tool for personal growth, enabling you to break free from the confines of routine and explore new horizons. It encourages you to live in the present, to savor the moment, and to embrace the uncertainty of the future.

Creating a Space that Reflects You, Not a Home that Demands You: Homeownership often carries the pressure of making decisions that will impact your life for decades to come. From paint colors to landscaping, every choice feels like a permanent commitment. This can lead to a sense of obligation, a feeling of being trapped in a space that may not truly reflect your evolving tastes and preferences. As a renter, you have the freedom to create a space that is truly yours, a reflection of your personality and your passions. You can decorate, rearrange furniture, and personalize your surroundings with minimal commitment. This freedom to express yourself without long-term consequences fosters a sense of creativity, individuality, and ownership, even within a temporary setting.

3. **Redefining Your Identity Beyond Homeownership:**

In a society that often equates homeownership with success, renting can challenge conventional norms and force you to redefine your definition of success. It encourages you to prioritize personal growth and experiences over material possessions, to focus on building a fulfilling life rather than simply accumulating assets.

This shift in perspective can be empowering. It frees you from the pressure of societal expectations and allows you to forge your own path, to define your own values and priorities. It's a reminder that success is not solely measured by the size of your house or the amount of equity you possess.

4. **Embracing the Journey, Not Just the Destination:**

Homeownership often feels like a destination, a final stage in a life journey. It can create the illusion that once you've achieved this goal, you've reached the peak of success, that the rest of your life is simply about maintaining your current status quo. Renting challenges this notion, reminding you that life is a constant journey, a series of chapters, each offering its own unique experiences and opportunities for growth. It encourages you to embrace change, to be adaptable, and to see each stage of life as a stepping stone towards something even greater.

The psychological benefits of renting extend far beyond simply saving money. They offer a pathway to self-discovery, personal liberation, and a deeper understanding of what truly matters in life. It's about living intentionally, choosing experiences over possessions, and embracing the freedom to create your own unique story, one chapter at a time.

Work To Live Or Live To Work

We all come to the same conclusions: life without happiness is worthless. If work-life is a balance of priorities, it sounds like you are likely to work to live. It's the key that unlocks doors beyond dreams to the challenges of life.

Ten Best Cities For Jobs

10 Orlando, FL

Total score	**60.95**
Job market rank	14
Socio-economics rank	37

Orlando, Florida ranked 10th for best cities for jobs in 2025.

9 Tempe, AZ

Total score	**61.03**
Job market rank	17
Socio-economics rank	22

Tempe, Arizona ranked 9th for best cities for jobs in 2025.

8 Washington, DC

Total score	**61.07**
Job market rank	11
Socio-economics rank	36

Washington, D.C., ranked 8th for best cities for jobs in 2025.

7 Chandler, AZ

Total score	**61.13**
Job market rank	15
Socio-economics rank	29

Chandler, Arizona ranked 7th for best cities for jobs in 2025.

6 Charleston, SC

Total score	**61.72**
Job market rank	6
Socio-economics rank	40

Charleston, South Carolina ranked 6th for best cities for jobs in 2025.

5 Portland, ME

Total score	64.29
Job market rank	5
Socio-economics rank	15

Portland, Maine ranked 5th for best cities for jobs in 2025.

4 South Burlington, VT

Total score	65.33
Job market rank	4
Socio-economics rank	5

South Burlington, Vermont ranked 4th for best cities for jobs in 2025.

3 Columbia, MD

Total score	66.38
Job market rank	2
Socio-economics rank	11

Columbia, Maryland ranked 3rd for best cities for jobs in 2025.

2 Pittsburgh, PA

Total score	**66.48**
Job market rank	3
Socio-economics rank	2

Pittsburgh, Pennsylvania ranked 2nd for best cities for jobs in 2025.

1 Scottsdale, AZ

Total score	**67.04**
Job market rank	1
Socio-economics rank	10

Scottsdale, Arizona ranked 1st for best cities for jobs in 2025.

Worst cities for jobs in 2025

10 Shreveport, LA

Total score	**44.36**
Job market rank	168
Socio-economics rank	176

Shreveport, Louisiana ranked 10th for worst cities for jobs in 2025.

9 Stockton, CA

Total score	**44.17**
Job market rank	173
Socio-economics rank	154

Stockton, California ranked 9th for worst cities for jobs in 2025.

8 Huntington, WV

Total score	**43.76**
Job market rank	182
Socio-economics rank	109

Huntington, West Virginia ranked 8th for worst cities for jobs in 2025.

7 Bakersfield, CA

Total score	**43.51**
Job market rank	180
Socio-economics rank	147

Bakersfield, California ranked 7th for worst cities for jobs in 2025.

6 Gulfport, MS

Total score	**43.13**
Job market rank	170
Socio-economics rank	179

Gulfport, Mississippi ranked 6th for worst cities for jobs in 2025.

5 Baton Rouge, LA

Total score	**42.71**
Job market rank	179
Socio-economics rank	167

Baton Rouge, Louisiana ranked 5th for worst cities for jobs in 2025.

4 Augusta, GA

Total score	**42.6**
Job market rank	178
Socio-economics rank	174

August, Georgia ranked 4th for worst cities for jobs in 2025.

3 San Bernardino, CA

Total score	**42.41**
Job market rank	175
Socio-economics rank	173

San Bernardino, California ranked 3rd for worst cities for jobs in 2025.

2 Detroit, MI

Total score	**41.44**
Job market rank	176
Socio-economics rank	178

Detroit, Michigan ranked 2nd for worst cities for jobs in 2025.

1 Memphis, TN

Total score	**40.77**
Job market rank	174
Socio-economics rank	182

Memphis, Tennessee ranked 1st for worst cities for jobs in 2025.

WANDERLUST

New York
SORRENTO
GENOVA
Conte Verde
Praha
Stuttgart
Baden-Württemberg
MAMOUNIA

3

EXPLORING ALTERNATIVE LIFESTYLES

Imagine trading in your mortgage payments for the open road, the wind whipping through your hair as you cruise towards the next adventure. This is the allure of RV living, a lifestyle that offers a unique blend of freedom, affordability, and a constant sense of discovery. It's a choice that's gaining traction, particularly among those seeking an escape from the traditional homeownership model, yearning for a more nomadic and less conventional existence.

Let's delve into the world of RV living and unpack the financial advantages that make it a compelling alternative. First and foremost, RV living offers a significant cost reduction compared to traditional homeownership. The initial investment in an RV can be a fraction of the cost of a house, especially when considering the price tags of homes in desirable locations. Moreover, the monthly expenses associated with RV living are significantly lower than mortgage payments, property taxes, and homeowners insurance.

The nomadic nature of RV living allows for a flexible lifestyle. You can choose to travel during the off-season, when prices for campsites and attractions are lower, maximizing your travel budget. Imagine waking up to breathtaking mountain views one day and enjoying the ocean breeze the next. You can adapt your travel plans to suit your desires and budget.

But the financial benefits of RV living extend beyond just cost savings. The lifestyle often fosters a sense of minimalism, prompting you to shed the excess baggage of material possessions. This shift in perspective can lead to a more fulfilling life centered around experiences rather than material wealth.

However, it's essential to acknowledge that RV living is not without its challenges. The initial purchase price of an RV can be a significant investment, and there are ongoing maintenance costs to factor in. You'll need to invest in the necessary equipment, accessories, and supplies to ensure comfortable and safe travels. Additionally, finding reliable parking spots and securing access to amenities, such as electricity and water, can sometimes be a logistical challenge.

The key to successful RV living lies in meticulous planning and a realistic assessment of your financial situation. Before embarking on this adventure, you need to consider the initial purchase price of the RV, the monthly expenses associated with travel and maintenance, and the potential for unforeseen costs.

Here's a step-by-step guide to help you navigate the financial aspects of RV living:

1. **Determine Your Budget:**

Initial Investment: Research different RV models, sizes, and features to determine your price range. Consider the cost of new versus used RVs and factor in potential upgrades and modifications.

Monthly Expenses: Estimate your monthly expenses, including:

Fuel: Calculate your estimated fuel consumption based on your travel plans and RV size.

Campground Fees: Research campground fees in your preferred destinations and consider options like state park campgrounds, private RV resorts, or boondocking (free camping).

Utilities: Factor in the cost of electricity, water, and sewer hookups, especially when staying in campgrounds.

Maintenance and Repairs: Set aside a budget for routine maintenance, repairs, and unexpected breakdowns.

Food and Supplies: Estimate your grocery expenses, supplies, and other essentials. **Entertainment**: Factor in the cost of activities, attractions, and entertainment while traveling.

Contingency Fund: Create a dedicated emergency fund to cover unforeseen expenses, such as medical emergencies or unexpected repairs.

2. **Explore Funding Options:**

Cash Savings: If you have substantial cash savings, you can purchase your RV outright, avoiding loan payments and interest charges.

RV Loans: Explore financing options from banks, credit unions, or RV dealerships. Compare interest rates, loan terms, and fees.

Personal Loans: Consider a personal loan if you need additional funds for your RV purchase or renovations.

Sell Existing Assets: If you own a home or other assets, consider selling them to free up capital for your RV investment.

3. **Downsizing and Simplifying:**

Minimalist Lifestyle: Embrace a minimalist lifestyle and declutter your belongings. Sell unwanted items to reduce your expenses and lighten your load for travel.

Digital Nomadism: Explore the possibility of remote work, allowing you to generate income while traveling.

4. **Embrace the Community:**

RV Clubs and Forums: Join RV clubs and online forums to connect with experienced RVers, exchange tips, and find resources.

RV Parks and Resorts: Take advantage of RV parks and resorts, which often offer amenities like laundry facilities, swimming pools, and social events.

5. **Maintain a Realistic Perspective:**

Flexibility and Adaptability: Be prepared to adjust your travel plans and adapt to unexpected situations.

Safety and Security: Prioritize your safety and security while traveling. Learn about RV safety tips, secure your RV, and be aware of your surroundings.

Financial Planning: Maintain a detailed budget and track your expenses to ensure you stay on track with your financial goals.

RV living presents an opportunity to embrace a more flexible, cost-effective, and experience-driven lifestyle. By carefully planning your finances and embracing the nomadic spirit, you can set yourself up for an adventure-filled journey that will create lasting memories. Remember, the road less traveled often leads to the most rewarding experiences.

Mobile home communities, often referred to as manufactured housing communities, offer a unique living experience that can be both appealing and challenging. These communities provide a sense of community and affordability, but they come with their own set of rules, regulations, and potential downsides.

Let's delve into the world of mobile homes, exploring the advantages and disadvantages of choosing this alternative lifestyle.

The Appeal of Mobile Home Living

For many individuals and families, mobile home communities present a compelling alternative to traditional homeownership. Here's why:

Affordability: Mobile homes are generally less expensive to purchase than traditional single-family homes. This affordability can be a significant draw for individuals on a tight budget, particularly those seeking to own their living space.

Lower Maintenance: Mobile homes often have lower maintenance requirements compared to traditional homes. This can translate to significant cost savings over the long term.

Community Living: Mobile home communities foster a sense of community, where residents often share common interests and participate in social activities. These communities can provide a welcoming environment for those seeking social connection and belonging.

Amenities: Many mobile home communities offer amenities like swimming pools, clubhouses, and recreational areas. These amenities can enhance the quality of life and provide opportunities for residents to engage in activities.

The Challenges of Mobile Home Living

While mobile home communities offer benefits, it's crucial to acknowledge the potential drawbacks before making a decision:

Property Value: Mobile homes are often considered less valuable than traditional homes, which can make it difficult to sell and can limit equity growth. This can also affect loan terms and insurance costs.

Land Lease Agreements: Most mobile homes are situated on leased land. This means residents pay monthly lease fees, which can increase over time and create uncertainty about the future of the property.

Community Rules: Mobile home communities typically have strict rules and regulations governing everything from landscaping to pet ownership. These rules can restrict personal freedom and potentially lead to conflicts with community management.

Maintenance Concerns: While maintenance is generally lower for mobile homes, it's important to recognize that older models can require more upkeep and repairs. This can add unforeseen expenses to the budget.

Location: Mobile home communities are often located in more rural or suburban areas, which can limit access to amenities like public transportation, shopping centers, and job opportunities.

Weighing the Pros and Cons

To determine if a mobile home community is the right fit for you, carefully consider both the advantages and disadvantages:

Affordability: If your top priority is finding a home that fits your budget, a mobile home community might be a viable option.

Community: If you desire a close-knit community and social connections, mobile home communities can offer a welcoming environment.

Location: Think about your desired proximity to work, schools, shopping, and other amenities. Mobile home communities are often located in more remote areas, so consider your commuting needs.

Maintenance: Factor in the potential costs of maintenance and repairs. If you're comfortable with DIY projects, a mobile home might be a good choice.

Property Value: Be aware that mobile homes may have limited appreciation potential. Consider your long-term housing goals and the implications of selling the property. Making an Informed Decision

Before committing to a mobile home community, it's essential to conduct thorough research and due diligence:

Visit Different Communities: Tour various communities and speak with residents to get a sense of their experiences and the atmosphere.

Review Community Rules: Carefully read and understand the community's rules and regulations.

Inspect the Mobile Home: Get a professional inspection to assess the condition of the mobile home and identify any potential repairs.

Research Land Lease Agreements: Understand the terms and conditions of the land lease agreement, including fees and potential future increases.

Consider Your Financial Situation: Carefully evaluate your budget and financial capacity to handle monthly lease payments, potential repairs, and future property value considerations.

Navigating the Mobile Home Market

Here are some additional tips for navigating the mobile home market:

Work with a Real Estate Agent: A knowledgeable real estate agent can help you find the right mobile home community and negotiate a fair price.

Research Financing Options: Explore financing options specific to manufactured housing, as these may differ from traditional mortgages.

Consult with a Financial Advisor: A financial advisor can help you determine if mobile home living aligns with your financial goals and long-term plans.

Conclusion

Mobile home communities offer a unique living experience with both advantages and disadvantages. For those seeking affordability, community living, and lower maintenance requirements, they can be a good option. However, it's essential to understand the potential downsides, such as property value limitations, land lease agreements, and community rules. By conducting thorough research, weighing the pros and cons, and carefully considering your needs and financial situation, you can make an informed decision about whether a mobile home community is the right fit for you. Remember, living in a mobile home community can be a positive and fulfilling experience when approached with careful consideration and planning.

The simplicity of camping and minimal living can be a liberating experience, offering a refreshing perspective on life and finances. Camping, in its purest form, embodies the essence of minimalism—a way of living that prioritizes experiences over material possessions. When you pitch your tent under the starry sky, you're not burdened by the weight of a mortgage, property taxes, or the constant pressure to upgrade your belongings. Instead, you're surrounded by nature's beauty, enjoying the company of loved ones, and embracing the simplicity of life's essentials.

Imagine waking up to the sounds of birds chirping, the gentle rustling of leaves, and the fresh scent of pine needles. The air is crisp, and the sun warms your skin as you prepare a simple breakfast over an open fire. You don't need a fancy coffee machine or a gourmet kitchen to enjoy a delicious meal; a campfire and a few basic ingredients are all you need. In this setting, your worries about work, deadlines, and the relentless pursuit of wealth fade away. You are present in the moment, appreciating the beauty of nature and the simple pleasures of life.

Camping allows you to reconnect with your inner self and rediscover the joy of living in harmony with nature. It's a reminder that true happiness doesn't come from accumulating things but from experiencing life's simple joys—the warmth of a campfire, the laughter of friends, and the beauty of a starry night. This minimalist approach to living extends beyond just camping. It's about recognizing that we don't need an abundance of material possessions to be happy. It's about prioritizing experiences over things, relationships over possessions, and quality over quantity.

In the realm of camping, the minimalist lifestyle isn't just a choice; it's a necessity. You learn to live with less, to pack light, and to appreciate the value of every item you carry. Every piece of gear you bring serves a purpose, and every item you leave behind represents freedom—freedom from unnecessary clutter, freedom from the burden of ownership, and freedom to experience life in its simplest form. Camping is a powerful reminder that happiness is not found in the pursuit of material wealth but in embracing the simple pleasures of life. It's a reminder that less is often more, and that true fulfillment comes from connecting with nature, with ourselves, and with loved ones.

The transition from a conventional lifestyle to a more minimalist one can be gradual and rewarding. Start with small changes—decluttering your home, getting rid of unused items, and focusing on experiences over possessions. You might discover that a minimalist lifestyle isn't a deprivation but a liberation. It's about letting go of the unnecessary and embracing the freedom that comes with living intentionally.

There Is No Greatness Where There Is No Simplicity

The Allure of Tiny Homes

As the minimalist movement gains momentum, tiny homes have emerged as a compelling alternative to traditional housing. These compact dwellings, often less than 500 square feet, are designed to maximize space efficiency and promote a simpler, more sustainable way of living.

The allure of tiny homes lies in their ability to free you from the financial constraints of traditional homeownership. By downsizing your living space, you can significantly reduce your mortgage payments, property taxes, utilities, and maintenance costs.

Tiny homes also offer a sense of freedom and flexibility. You can easily transport your home to different locations, allowing you to explore new places and experience different lifestyles.

This nomadic spirit is appealing to many who seek adventure and a break from the monotony of everyday life.

However, adopting a tiny home lifestyle isn't without its challenges. The limited space can be a significant adjustment, requiring careful planning and organization. You'll need to be creative in maximizing storage space and finding multi-functional furniture. It's essential to be realistic about your needs and priorities. If you enjoy entertaining guests or have a large family, a tiny home may not be the ideal solution. However, for individuals and couples seeking a simpler, more sustainable way of living, a tiny home can offer a unique and fulfilling lifestyle.

The Financial Advantages of Minimalism

Adopting a minimalist lifestyle, whether through camping or tiny homes, can have significant financial benefits. By embracing simplicity and reducing your material possessions, you can free up valuable resources and create more financial freedom.

Reducing Expenses:

Housing Costs: Camping and tiny homes offer significantly lower housing costs compared to traditional homeownership. You'll avoid the burden of mortgage payments, property taxes, insurance, and maintenance.

Utilities: With a smaller living space, your utility bills will be considerably lower. You'll consume less energy for heating, cooling, and lighting.

Transportation: Adopting a minimalist lifestyle often involves reducing car dependence, leading to lower transportation costs.

Food and Entertainment: You'll likely find yourself spending less on food and entertainment when you prioritize experiences over material possessions.

Increasing Savings:

Reduced Debt: By minimizing expenses, you can free up cash flow to pay down existing debts, such as credit card debt or student loans, faster.

Growing Savings: With lower expenses, you'll have more money to save for future goals, such as retirement, travel, or education.

Financial Flexibility: A minimalist lifestyle can provide greater financial flexibility, allowing you to pursue your passions and make choices that align with your values. Beyond the Financial Benefits:

The advantages of a minimalist lifestyle extend beyond the financial realm. Embracing simplicity can bring a sense of peace, contentment, and fulfillment.

Reduced Stress: Minimalism can help reduce stress by eliminating clutter and distractions, creating a more peaceful and organized living space.

Increased Focus: By prioritizing essential needs and reducing distractions, you can enhance your focus and concentration on what matters most.

Greater Time Freedom: Minimalism can free up your time by reducing chores, maintenance, and the need to acquire and manage possessions.

Increased Gratitude: Minimalism encourages gratitude for what you have, rather than longing for what you don't.

Finding Your Own Path to Minimalism

The transition to a minimalist lifestyle is a personal journey, and there's no single right way to do it. You can start with small changes and gradually embrace a more minimalist approach.

Decluttering: Begin by decluttering your home, getting rid of unused items and creating a more organized living space.

Mindful Shopping: Become more mindful of your purchases, considering whether you truly need an item before you buy it.

Experiences Over Possessions: Prioritize experiences over material possessions. Invest in travel, adventures, and activities that enrich your life.

Embrace the Joy of Simple Things: Rediscover the joy of simple things in life, such as spending time with loved ones, enjoying nature, and pursuing hobbies.

Minimalism is not about deprivation or sacrifice; it's about making intentional choices that align with your values and priorities. It's about freeing yourself from the burdens of consumerism and reclaiming control over your time, your resources, and your life. Whether you embrace a minimalist lifestyle through camping, tiny homes, or simply by making mindful choices, you can find a path to greater simplicity, financial freedom, and a more fulfilling life.

The allure of off-the-grid living is undeniable. It whispers promises of self-sufficiency, a connection to nature, and a life free from the constraints of modern society. The image of a cozy cabin nestled in a secluded forest, powered by solar panels and fueled by a garden bursting with fresh produce, is a tempting vision for many. But before you embrace the dream of living off the grid, it's crucial to understand the realities and financial implications that come with this lifestyle choice.

One of the most significant aspects of off-the-grid living is its reliance on alternative energy sources. While renewable energy is becoming increasingly accessible, it's not without its costs. Installing solar panels, wind turbines, or a hydroelectric system can require a substantial upfront investment. You'll need to factor in the initial purchase cost, installation fees, and ongoing maintenance. Additionally, the efficiency of these systems can vary depending on your location, weather conditions, and energy needs.

Beyond energy, you'll need to consider the cost of building or acquiring a suitable off-grid dwelling. If you're planning to construct your own home, you'll face a unique set of challenges. Obtaining permits and navigating local zoning regulations can be complex, especially in areas with limited access to infrastructure. Furthermore, transporting building materials and equipment to remote locations can add significantly to the expense. If you're considering purchasing an existing off-grid property, be prepared for thorough inspections and potential surprises, as these structures often require significant renovations and upgrades to meet your needs.

Living off the grid typically means becoming more self-reliant in terms of food production. Gardening and raising livestock can be rewarding and cost-effective, but they require a significant commitment of time and effort. You'll need to learn the basics of organic farming, livestock management, and food preservation. The initial investment in seeds, tools, fencing, and animal care can be considerable. Moreover, the success of your food production will depend heavily on your climate, soil conditions, and your experience in agriculture.

Water is another essential element for off-grid living. You'll need a reliable source of clean and safe drinking water. This could involve collecting rainwater, drilling a well, or purchasing water from a local source. Each option comes with its own costs and logistical challenges. Well drilling, for instance, can be expensive, and you'll need to factor in the cost of pumps, filters, and regular maintenance. Rainwater collection systems require proper installation and maintenance to prevent contamination.

Furthermore, you'll need to address waste management in a sustainable way. Living off the grid often means composting kitchen scraps and using a composting toilet system. While these methods are eco-friendly, they require proper setup and ongoing maintenance to avoid potential issues.

Aside from the tangible costs, there are also less obvious financial implications to consider. Living off the grid can be isolating, particularly for individuals seeking a social life. Access to healthcare and education might be limited in remote areas, potentially requiring you to travel long distances for essential services. You'll also need to factor in the cost of transportation, as off-the-grid living often involves relying on vehicles for shopping, social activities, and medical appointments.

The financial aspects of off-the-grid living go beyond mere expenses. It requires a shift in mindset towards financial independence and resourcefulness. You'll need to be comfortable with budgeting, financial planning, and potentially learning new skills to make your living situation sustainable.

However, the potential benefits of off-the-grid living are not to be dismissed. For those seeking a simpler, more sustainable lifestyle, it can be a profoundly rewarding experience. The connection to nature, the sense of self-reliance, and the freedom from the pressures of modern society can be deeply fulfilling.

Before embarking on this path, it's important to weigh the pros and cons carefully.

Ask yourself:

Am I prepared for the financial challenges? Off-the-grid living requires a significant upfront investment and ongoing financial management. Are you comfortable with the potential risks and uncertainties?

Do I possess the necessary skills and knowledge? Living off the grid requires a variety of skills, including gardening, DIY repairs, and energy management. Are you willing to learn these skills or have access to the resources that can support you?

What is my level of commitment? Off-the-grid living is not a temporary escape; it's a lifestyle choice that demands dedication and flexibility. Are you willing to commit to this lifestyle in the long term?

If you're drawn to the idea of off-the-grid living, thorough research is essential. Connect with individuals who have already embarked on this path, visit off-the-grid communities, and explore resources on sustainable living. By understanding the financial implications and challenges, you can make an informed decision that aligns with your values, resources, and aspirations.

Ultimately, the decision of whether or not off-the-grid living is right for you is a personal one. But by carefully considering the financial aspects and other considerations, you can make a choice that empowers you to live a fulfilling and sustainable life.

The Challenges Of Condominium Lifestyle

For some home hunters the thought of maintaining an entire house and yard conjures up a bit of anxiety. The cost can send shivers down your budget spine

While cohousing offers many financial benefits, it's crucial to be aware of potential challenges before making a decision:

Community living is gaining traction, offering an alternative to traditional homeownership with a strong emphasis on shared spaces and community building. Cohousing communities are intentionally designed neighborhoods where residents share common facilities, such as kitchens, dining rooms, laundry rooms, and recreational areas. The idea is to create a sense of belonging and mutual support, while also reducing individual costs associated with homeownership.

Imagine a scenario where you own your own private living space, but have access to a communal kitchen equipped with top-of-the-line appliances, a cozy common room for gatherings, and a shared garden for fresh produce. This is the essence of cohousing. Residents often participate in decision-making processes, contributing to a sense of ownership and collective well-being.

Financial Benefits of Cohousing or better known as Condominium living

This can offer significant financial advantages, especially for those looking to downsize, retire, or simply live more sustainably. Here's a breakdown of the key cost-saving aspects:

Shared Ownership and Costs: By sharing common facilities, residents collectively reduce individual expenses. This includes costs for construction, maintenance, utilities, and insurance.

This shared approach leads to significant savings compared to individual homeownership.

Smaller Living Spaces: Cohousing communities often prioritize smaller, more efficient living spaces, minimizing the overall cost of construction and maintenance. This is a wise approach for individuals or couples who value a simpler lifestyle and prioritize community over expansive living areas.

Reduced Energy Consumption: Shared facilities like laundry rooms and kitchens can lead to reduced energy consumption per individual. The efficient use of resources and shared appliances can lower utility bills.

Collaborative Maintenance: Cohousing communities encourage residents to participate in maintenance tasks. This collective effort can minimize the need for expensive professional contractors and reduce individual responsibilities.

Access to Community Resources: By sharing resources like tools, vehicles, and knowledge, residents can avoid individual purchases and rely on collective expertise.

Community Fit: Cohousing communities often have strict guidelines and a strong emphasis on shared values. It's essential to find a community that aligns with your personal preferences and lifestyle.

Shared Decision-Making: Residents actively participate in community decisions. This can lead to occasional disagreements and the need for compromise.

Privacy Concerns: While cohousing offers a strong sense of community, it's important to consider your need for privacy. Shared spaces and close proximity can sometimes limit personal autonomy.

Limited Availability: Cohousing communities are not as widespread as traditional neighborhoods, limiting your choices in terms of location and availability.

Finding Your Cohousing Community

If you're intrigued by the cohousing lifestyle, here's how to explore your options:

Research Online: Numerous websites and organizations dedicated to cohousing provide information, resources, and listings of communities across the country.

Connect with Cohousing Groups: Many local communities have cohousing groups or associations. These groups can provide insights, answer questions, and offer opportunities to network with like-minded individuals.

Visit Cohousing Communities: Don't hesitate to schedule visits to cohousing communities that pique your interest. This allows you to observe firsthand the lifestyle, meet residents, and assess whether the community is a good fit for you.

Benefits Beyond Finances

Cohousing is not just about cost savings; it's about cultivating a sense of belonging, mutual support, and shared purpose. The community aspect of cohousing can be profoundly rewarding, fostering friendships, reducing loneliness, and creating a supportive environment for individuals of all ages.

Cohousing communities often promote sustainable living practices, encouraging residents to embrace eco-friendly habits, conserve resources, and connect with their neighbors. This commitment to community and sustainability can lead to a fulfilling and meaningful lifestyle.

A Lifestyle Choice, Not Just a Financial Decision

Cohousing is a lifestyle choice that demands careful consideration, but for those seeking a more connected and fulfilling way of life, it can be a fulfilling path. By embracing shared values, resources, and responsibilities, cohousing communities foster a sense of community, environmental stewardship, and financial security. While cohousing is not for everyone, it offers a viable alternative to traditional homeownership for those who value community, shared spaces, and a sustainable lifestyle. By exploring the world of cohousing, you may discover a fulfilling way to live that aligns with your financial and personal goals.

The Challenge of Measuring Success

Will a luxury house or condo that comes with a sizzling car or a stuffed bank account bring perfection to your life?

Many of you will say "yes" and you are not wrong. We can buy anything with money. A luxury house can give you a sense of satisfaction and a handsome-looking vehicle can change your status in the eyes of others. But what if you don't feel content after having all this? We all come to the same conclusions: life without happiness is worthless.

There are so many varieties of lifestyles to choose from.

The choice is yours.

Challenges of RV Living

The RV industry offers potential buyers several sizes of vehicles separated into different categories or "classes." A Class A model is a large, traditional motorhome that can range in length from 26 to 45 feet and weigh upwards of 15 tons. These coaches often resemble buses and are usually the largest motorized models on the road. Meanwhile, a Class C is a mid-sized option that is typically between 20 and 30 feet long and weighs about 10,000 pounds or so, although there are larger options as well. Both of these classes are built on large chassis that allow for more living space, usually at the expense of maneuverability and gas mileage.

A Class B RV rides on a van chassis, making them more approachable to newcomers and offering better fuel economy. Naturally, these vehicles have less interior space but still provide a surprising number of features and amenities. Most camper vans are built on the Mercedes Sprinter, Ford Transit, or Ram ProMaster platforms. Each of those models has its pros and cons, with varying levels of performance and features at different price points. Generally speaking, the Sprinter is the priciest of the three, while the ProMaster is the most affordable. The Ford Transit usually slots in somewhere in the middle.

One of the significant benefits of a camper van is that it can often go places that the larger models struggle to reach. Some models come with all-wheel-drive, for instance, allowing them to handle off-road conditions that could be detrimental to Class A and C RVs. Camper vans also fit into smaller campsites, are easier to drive on narrow, twisty roads, and can even be parked in some garages. Those capabilities make them very appealing to many RVers.

The Best Class B Camper Vans of 2025

If you're shopping for a camper van, these are the models to keep on your shortlist. Each has its own unique personality and capabilities so it's important to check them out in person and even take them for a test drive. Despite being smaller than a Class A or C, a Class B van is still a significant investment, so you'll want to be sure you're picking the right one for you.

Winnebago Revel

The diesel-powered Winnebago Revel rides on the Mercedes Sprinter chassis, giving it excellent performance on-road and off. The vehicle's 3-liter turbo engine provides smooth, steady acceleration with reliable power and fuel efficiency. And when you're ready to drive to a remote campsite, this van has you covered too. It comes with on-demand all-wheel drive, a rugged suspension, high and low gearing, and hill-descent assist.

Once you get to your campsite, the Revel has plenty of features to keep you comfortable. Those include an 8.4kWh Lithionics battery that can be recharged using the van's dual-alternator system or a 210W roof-mounted solar panel. The Class B comes with a hydronic heating system, screen doors on the side and back, and a Bluetooth-controlled powered awning with LED lighting. Solar panels and an air conditioner are optional add-ons.

Winnebago didn't skimp on the interior features, either. The Revel has a galley kitchen with a single burner induction stove, a stainless steel sink, and a 3 cubic-foot refrigerator/freezer. A full-size bed comfortably sleeps two and lifts out of the way when not in use to reveal a gear garage with ample storage space. The van even has a shower and cassette toilet, as well as fresh and gray water tanks. MSRP: $254,076

Winnebago Revel Sport

While the classic Winnebago Revel is a great option for most travelers, the Revel Sport offers amazing features for those who prefer to wander a little further afield. This model is built to take on even more rugged off-road conditions and comes with boondocking capabilities for extended off-grid camping.

Like its sibling, the Revel Sport rides on the AWD Mercedes Sprinter chassis, utilizing a 2.0L turbo-diesel engine that provides plenty of power and torque. The van offers 8″of ground clearance and is about 4″narrower than the standard Revel, making it a bit more nimble both on and off pavement. And thanks to a 4.1kWh Lithionics battery, combined with alternator charging and a 215W solar panel, it is well suited for camping off-grid. The Revel Sport also comes with a larger gear garage, as well as a versatile modular rack that makes it easy to add additional accessories and carry more gear.

Inside, the two camper vans offer similar designs, with a few subtle differences. For instance, the Sport comes with a lounge area that includes a pedestal table and a two-seat dinette just behind the pivoting driver's seat. The galley kitchen offers options for indoor and outdoor cooking, thanks to a fold-down table and a portable induction stove. A mini-fridge is accessible from both the interior and exterior, while a countertop extension adds additional space for meal prep. A power lift bed, hydronic heating, and a wet bath with cassette toilet round out the features. Best of all, the Revel Sport has a more approachable starting price with an MSRP of $210,570

Thor Motor Coach Sequence

Built on the Ram ProMaster platform, the Thor Motor Coach Sequence is one of the most fuel-efficient Class B models on the market. The van's gas-sipping V6 engine delivers plenty of power for cruising at highway speeds, delivering a comfortable ride in a spacious vehicle that isn't overwhelmingly large.

The exterior of the Sequence comes with a built-in patio awning complete with LED lights and a retractable rooftop tent sleeping area. The van comes with a 200-watt solar panel that connects to a 3,000-watt inverter and a 2,800W Onan generator. It even has a built-in Thule bike rack for hauling two adult bicycles.

Inside, the camper van comfortably sleeps two and has an array of outstanding features. Those include a two-burner gas stove, a convection microwave oven, a stainless-steel sink, and a 12-volt electric refrigerator. The Sequence's living room comes with a comfortable couch—that converts to a bed—a smart TV, LED lighting, and durable, easy-to-clean vinyl flooring. It even ships with a Winegard Connect 2.0 signal booster that functions as a 4G internet hotpot, Wi-Fi router, and over-the-air TV antenna. MSRP: $148,120

Airstream Rangeline

Did you know that in addition to making its iconic aluminum travel trailers, Airstream also makes camper vans? The Rangeline model brings the company's famous build quality and attention to detail to the Class B market. Best of all, this well-appointed RV has a surprisingly affordable price tag.

Based on the Ram ProMaster platform, the Rangeline features a fuel-efficient 3.6L V6 engine with 276 horsepower and 250 lb-ft of torque, and a towing capacity of 3,500 pounds. The van comes with an air conditioner, hydronic furnace and hot water system, as well as heated black and gray water tanks. These features make it a good option for year-round camping, even in colder conditions.

The Rangeline's interior includes plenty of amenities too. For instance, it has a versatile table set-up perfect for meals or working on the road. And when not in use, the table can be removed altogether to free up additional space. The van's galley kitchen has a 3.2-cubic-foot mini-refrigerator/freezer, a microwave oven, and a portable 1,000-watt induction cooktop. A full-size bed comes standard, while a pop-up roof tent is an optional add-on. And for those looking to do a little boondocking, the van ships with a 200-watt solar panel, 2,000-watt inverter, and 270 amp-hour lithium battery pack. MSRP: $157,500

Pleasure-Way Plateau XLTS

When you're shopping for a Class B camper van, many of the models can start to look the same after a while. That isn't a problem with the Pleasure-Way Plateau XLTS, which has its own distinct look inside and out. This is the brand's flagship model, bringing upscale features and luxury sensibilities to a vehicle that is still maneuverable and easy to drive.

The exterior of the Plateau XLTS is a little boxier than most other Class B models, but that pays off with a roomier, more open interior. You'll be amazed at how less cramped this van feels compared to others, offering enough room for an efficient galley kitchen that includes a single-basin sink, a built-in induction cooktop, and a mini-fridge. A large sofa serves as a lounge area and a dinette with a removable table. That same couch converts to a massive memory foam bed when you're ready to call it a day, while the onboard dry bath—complete with a walk-in shower—is a true standout in this space.

Pleasure-WayThis camper van is a bit of a technical wonder, too. It comes standard with 500W of solar, has a 600Ah house battery, and a 3000W inverter. A 10″ touchscreen control panel provides access to all of the van's heating, cooling, and lighting functionality, as well as the powered awning and the 2.5kW auto-start generator. A Truma AquaGo water heater provides instant hot water at all times, while all of the onboard appliances and components are designed to efficiently sip energy, allowing for longer off-grid camping. But don't worry, when you're boondocking, you won't exactly be roughing it. This is one of the most comfortable and relaxing Class B models on the market today. MSRP: $230,750

Tiffin GH1 Adventure Van

Tiffin bills its GH1 as the "ultimate adventure van platform," and it backs up that claim with some impressive features. Like many of the other options on this list, this Class B model uses the AWD Mercedes Sprinter as its platform, along with a set of BFGoodrich all-terrain tires, instantly giving it outstanding off-road cred. A set of Fox shock absorbers, a rugged suspension, and all-terrain tires only further enhance those capabilities, making this one of the best options for camping at remote locations.

The GH1's off-grid camping prowess is further enhanced by a 540Ah Battleborn house battery system connected to a 3,000W Victron inverter. The van also features 220W solar panels, and comes with a hydronic heater and a 15,000 BTU air conditioner for camping in all seasons. A powered patio awning extends the living space outdoors, where you'll also find LED patio lighting, illuminated low-profile running boards, and a factory-installed light bar. A fixed side-mounted ladder provides access to a burly roof rack.

Inside, the GH1 is no less impressive. The van features a dinette with a removable swivel table, solid surface countertops, and wooden cabinetry. The kitchen is outfitted with a 12V mini-fridge, portable single-burner induction cooktop, a stainless steel sink, and a removable bamboo counter extension. The onboard wet bath includes a shower and a cassette toilet, and converts to a closet when not in use. The van comes with LED mood lighting throughout, and has a primary sleep space mounted on a power lift system with a gear garage located underneath. MSRP: $238,496

Grand Design Lineage Series VT

Grand Design's move into the motorized RV space has been impressive, bringing excellent design and engineering to the space. That includes the all-new Lineage Series VT model, a Class B van that brings some excellent new features and innovative technology. That includes an industry-first stealth split A/C system that cleverly moves the 20,000 BTU air conditioner off the roof and under the floor, where it delivers unprecedented cooling power with virtually no sound.

When building its first-ever camper van, Grand Design went with the Ford Transit chassis and included all-wheel-drive standard from the factory. The rig comes with a Raptor-inspired front grill that gives it an aggressive and rugged look befitting an adventure van. It also has an optional pop-top option—a first for Ford Transit—that allows it to comfortably sleep four. Add in a 165Ah house battery and 400W solar standard, and you have plenty of versatility for off-grid exploration. Need more power? Customers can opt to double the battery size and add 300W of additional solar on the pop-top or 700W via the awning.

As you would expect from Grand Design, the interior is well designed, comfortable, and built with high-quality materials. A plush bed is found at the back of the van, with a gear garage located underneath. The rig also includes an onboard shower, an integrated induction stove, and a 12V 3.2-cubic-foot refrigerator. But perhaps the most impressive—and unexpected—amenity is the entertainment center that includes a motorized screen and built-in projector. MSRP: $216,613

Entegra Coach Launch

If you're looking for a luxurious Class B that is still rugged enough to go anywhere, the Entegra Coach Launch is the model for you. This vehicle is built on the Sprinter platform, which means it has on-demand AWD and a powerful 3.0L V6 engine for on and off-road travel. It also features upgraded shocks and a heavy-duty stabilizer bar, along with BFGoodrich all-terrain tires for a smooth journey no matter where your adventures take you.

Once at the campsite, you can deploy the armless patio awning that includes an LED light strip and built-in wind sensor, which automatically retracts if conditions get to harsh. The van also comes with a double roof rack for hauling gear and a roof-mounted 200-watt solar panel. An exterior fold-out table, a screen door on the entrance, and a moveable ladder are also standard equipment. We also appreciate the 17,000 BTU hydronic heater, and 13,500 BTU A/C unit, which keep the interior comfortable in a variety of environments.

The interior of the Launch offers even more amenities. Its kitchen features a dinette with a collapsible table, a 3-cubic-foot refrigerator, a portable induction stove, and a stainless steel sink. A full-size drop-down bed comfortably sleeps two and sits over a cavernous gear garage for storing your equipment. Meanwhile, the onboard wet bath includes a shower, a cassette toilet, a roof vent, and a removable bamboo shelf. Everything from the cabinetry to the furniture to the LED lighting is top-notch, with fantastic quality throughout. MSRP: $209,993

Coachmen Beyond

The Coachmen Beyond camper van utilizes the Ford Transit chassis for its underpinnings, which makes it a very efficient and comfortable vehicle. Powered by Ford's incredibly reliable 3.5L EcoBoost engine and a ten-speed transmission, this model handles remarkably well, inspiring confidence wherever you go. It also comes with the automaker's full suite of Co-

Pilot360 technology, which includes adaptive cruise control, blind spot monitoring, front and rear camera systems, and lane-keep assist.

Standard exterior equipment includes a 195W solar panel, a 2.8 kWh generator, rear and side screen doors, and a built-in Wi-Fi signal booster. The camper van comes with a 2,000W Xantrex inverter, an armless motion-sensing side awning, and a Supersprings suspension kit. Optional add-ons include a 640Ah lithium battery pack with internal heater, a Truma A/C unit, and gray tank heaters to extend the camping season

Inside, the Beyond comes with a couch that converts into two twin beds, a Firefly multiplexing system, and a Truma Combi Eco Plus furnace and water heater. The kitchenette has an induction cooktop, microwave, 12-volt refrigerator, and sink. Meanwhile, the onboard bathroom includes a Shower Miser water saver paired with a hand-held shower head, flip-down sink, and a cassette toilet. Hardwood cabinetry adds further convenience and elegance. This van is one of the more affordable on this list, too, with an MSRP: that starts at $149,999.

Winnebago Solis

The Winnebago Solis is one of the most versatile Class B RVs on the market, with two cozy floor plans designed to support an active lifestyle. Built on the Ram ProMaster platform, this van is powered by a 280 horsepower, 3.6L V6 engine that feels comfortable and controlled both on highways and backroads. And with the the ability to sleep up to four people—thanks in part to a pop-up rooftop extension—you can bring more friends and family along on your adventures.Key features of the Solis include the aforementioned pop-up sleeping area on the roof, side and rear screen doors, roof vents, and underfloor storage. The van features heavy-duty vinyl flooring and LED lighting throughout and comes with a digital touch panel for monitoring essential systems. A Truma Combi Eco heating system is included, but air conditioning is an optional upgrade. A 2,800W gas generator is a standard feature, as is a 220-watt solar panel.The Solis' interior space comes outfitted with a two-burner cooktop with glass cover, a 3-cubic-foot refrigerator/freezer, a stainless-steel sink, and a spice rack. A Murphy bed provides additional sleeping space inside the vehicle, with hidden gear storage underneath. The van's wet bath has a cassette toilet and shower with an Eco-Hot water system. Ceiling-to-floor insulation keeps the space warm and quiet in a variety of weather conditions, while USB charging points are conveniently located around the cabin. MSRP: $156,254These are our picks for the best Class B camper vans currently available. Any one of these models makes a perfect travel companion. Which one is right for you comes down to personal needs, preferences, budget, and the features you want from an RV.

CHALLENGES TO FIND THE BEST PLACES TO LIVE

4

CHOOSING THE BEST LOCATION TO LIVE

As you embark on the quest for your ideal living space, one of the most crucial factors to consider is the cost of living and the amenities available in different locations.

These two elements, often intertwined, can significantly impact your overall quality of life and financial well-being. This section will serve as your compass, guiding you through the intricate landscape of evaluating the cost of living and amenities in different areas.

Think of it like planning a road trip. You wouldn't just jump into your car and drive without a map, would you? Similarly, approaching your search for the perfect location without understanding the cost of living and amenities would be like navigating a foreign city without a guide.

So, let's dive into the key aspects of assessing these crucial factors, transforming you from a clueless traveler into a seasoned explorer.

Cost of Living: Unveiling the Price Tags of Everyday Life

Imagine this: You've narrowed down your choices to a few promising locations, each seemingly offering its own unique charm. But before you let your heart get carried away, it's time to step back and analyze the financial realities. This is where understanding the cost of living comes into play.

Understanding the Basics

Cost of living refers to the average expenses incurred by individuals or households in a particular region. It encompasses a wide range of essential items and services, including:

- **Housing:** This is often the biggest chunk of your budget, encompassing rent, mortgage payments, property taxes, and utilities.
- **Transportation:** Factor in fuel costs, public transportation fares, car maintenance, and potential parking expenses.
- **Food:** Groceries, dining out, and take-out meals all contribute to your overall food expenditures.
- **Healthcare:** Medical insurance premiums, doctor's visits, and prescription drugs can add up quickly.
- **Education:** Consider the costs of schooling, tuition, and childcare for your children.

- **Entertainment:** Allocate a budget for your leisure activities, including movies, concerts, and dining out.

Unveiling the Hidden Costs

While the above categories represent the core components of the cost of living, it's crucial to remember that hidden costs often lurk beneath the surface. These can include:

- **State and Local Taxes:** Beyond federal income taxes, states and cities levy their own taxes, which can vary significantly across regions.
- **Insurance Premiums:** Auto insurance, homeowners insurance, and health insurance premiums can fluctuate greatly depending on your location.
- **Utility Costs:** Electricity, water, gas, and internet bills can vary significantly, often influenced by climate and energy regulations.
- **Membership Fees:** Consider the cost of gym memberships, recreational activities, or professional memberships.

The Power of Online Cost of Living Calculators

Luckily, you don't have to embark on this cost-of-living analysis alone. Online tools are available to help you crunch the numbers. Cost of living calculators allow you to compare the expenses of different locations based on your specific needs and preferences.

These calculators gather data from various sources and use complex algorithms to provide a comprehensive picture of the cost of living in different cities and towns. While these calculators are helpful starting points, they should be considered as estimates. Your actual expenses will depend on your individual lifestyle and choices.

Beyond Numbers: Assessing Amenities for a Thriving Life

While the cost of living paints a financial picture, it's essential to consider the amenities offered in different locations. Amenities can range from practical necessities to cultural experiences, shaping your daily life and overall well-being.

Essential Amenities for Everyday Life

Here are some essential amenities that you should consider:

- **Healthcare Access:** The availability and quality of healthcare services are crucial, particularly if you have health concerns.
- **Education Options:** If you have children, access to good schools is a top priority.
- **Transportation Infrastructure:** Efficient transportation networks, including public transport, can significantly impact your daily commute and travel experiences.
- **Grocery Stores and Restaurants:** Convenience and variety are crucial factors when evaluating access to groceries and dining options.

- **Public Parks and Green Spaces:** Outdoor spaces offer opportunities for recreation, relaxation, and community connection.

Cultural and Recreational Amenities for a Richer Life

Beyond the essentials, consider amenities that contribute to your overall well-being and enjoyment:

- **Cultural Institutions:** Museums, art galleries, theaters, and libraries provide opportunities for cultural enrichment.
- **Recreational Opportunities:** Parks, hiking trails, sports facilities, and recreational centers enhance your active lifestyle.
- **Social Activities:** Consider access to social events, community centers, and clubs that align with your interests.
- **Shopping and Dining:** Retail options, restaurants, and entertainment venues shape your lifestyle and social experiences.

Evaluating the Fit for Your Lifestyle

Now, armed with your understanding of the cost of living and amenities, it's time to find the perfect match for your unique lifestyle. Consider these key questions:

- What are your priorities? Do you prioritize affordability, access to quality healthcare, or proximity to cultural institutions?
- What is your desired lifestyle? Do you envision yourself living in a bustling city, a quiet suburb, or a rural area?
- What are your financial constraints? Your budget will play a significant role in shaping your choices.
- What are your long-term goals? Are you looking to raise a family, retire comfortably, or pursue a specific career path?

A Holistic Approach

Don't rely solely on data and online tools. It's crucial to experience potential locations firsthand. Visiting a few places you're considering can provide a deeper understanding of the atmosphere, culture, and amenities.

Talk to locals, explore neighborhoods, and try out different activities. This hands-on approach allows you to gain valuable insights that go beyond numbers and statistics.

The Search for Balance

Finding the perfect location involves striking a balance between the cost of living, amenities, and your personal priorities. It's about finding a place that not only fits your budget but also enhances your quality of life.

This journey of location exploration isn't just about finding an address. It's about discovering a place where you can thrive, connect, and build a fulfilling life.

Embrace the Journey

Remember, the search for the perfect location is a dynamic process. Don't be afraid to adjust your expectations, explore new possibilities, and embrace the journey.

As you navigate the landscape of cost of living and amenities, keep in mind that the ideal location is not a destination but a journey of discovery. You are not just finding a place to live, you're finding a place to belong.

The decision of where to live is deeply intertwined with your safety and sense of community. While the cost of living and amenities are important considerations, feeling safe and connected within your surroundings is crucial for a fulfilling and happy life.

It's about more than just avoiding crime; it's about finding a place where you feel a sense of belonging, where you can build meaningful relationships, and where you can contribute to a vibrant community.

This feeling of belonging is often reflected in the social fabric of a community. Strong community ties can foster a sense of shared responsibility and encourage neighbors to look out for each other. This can translate into lower crime rates, a more welcoming environment, and a sense of shared purpose that enriches your everyday life. You might find that in some neighborhoods, people are more likely to engage in friendly conversations, participate in local events, or help each other out in times of need.

For young professionals, the allure of bustling city centers can be tempting, but the potential for isolation in a fast-paced environment should not be overlooked. While cities offer a vibrant social scene and a wide range of opportunities, they can also be impersonal and even isolating for those seeking a sense of community. On the other hand, suburbs can provide a calmer atmosphere with more opportunities for interaction with neighbors. Consider joining local clubs, volunteering, or simply striking up conversations with people in your neighborhood.

For retirees, finding a community where they can connect with others of similar age and interests is essential. Retirement communities or towns with active senior centers can provide a sense of belonging and social interaction, offering opportunities for new friendships and shared experiences. This can be particularly crucial if you're moving to a new area where you don't know anyone.

For families, safety and community are paramount considerations. You want to ensure that your children can grow up in a safe and nurturing environment, with access to good schools, parks, and recreational activities. It's worth researching the crime rates and school performance in different areas before making a decision.

But how do you find the right balance between safety and community? Here are some practical tips:

Research crime statistics: Don't rely solely on anecdotal evidence; consult reliable data sources like the FBI's Uniform Crime Reporting program or local police departments.

Explore local forums and social media groups: Join online communities dedicated to specific areas to get a real-life perspective on safety and community.

Take a walk around the neighborhood: Get a feel for the atmosphere and the people who live there. Observe how people interact with each other and the level of activity in the area.

Attend local events and community meetings: This can give you an opportunity to interact with residents, learn about local issues, and assess the community's overall spirit.

Talk to residents: Engage in conversations with people who live in the area to gain insights into their experiences and perspectives.

Remember, safety and community are subjective experiences, and what feels safe and welcoming to one person might not feel the same to another. Ultimately, the best way to determine if an area is a good fit for you is to spend some time there and see for yourself.

Consider these scenarios:

1. **The city dweller:** Sarah, a young professional, had always envisioned herself living in a vibrant city. Her job offered flexibility, so she could choose where she wanted to live. She was drawn to the energy and

opportunities of the city, and she was excited about the diverse cultural experiences and nightlife that it offered. However, after several years of living in a bustling city, Sarah began to feel a sense of isolation. Her interactions with her neighbors were limited to brief greetings in the elevator or fleeting encounters on the street. She realized that the constant hustle and bustle of city life had made it difficult to form deep connections.

2. **The suburban family:** John and Mary, a young couple with two young children, were looking for a home in a safe and family-friendly community. They wanted a place where their children could grow up in a nurturing environment, with access to good schools and recreational activities. They decided to settle in a quiet suburban neighborhood, drawn by the promise of a safe and peaceful life. However, they soon discovered that life in the suburbs could be just as isolating as city life, especially for young families. The lack of public transportation made it difficult to get around, and the lack of a vibrant social scene left them feeling disconnected from the community.
3. **The retired couple:** Bob and Carol, a retired couple, had always dreamed of living in a warm and sunny place with a close-knit community. They decided to relocate to a small town in Florida, hoping to find a place where they could enjoy their retirement years in peace. They quickly integrated into the community, making friends at the local senior center and joining clubs and organizations. They

found that the small town offered a sense of belonging and camaraderie, and they enjoyed the leisurely pace of life.

These examples illustrate the diversity of experiences that people have when it comes to safety and community. While cities can offer a vibrant social scene, they can also be isolating. Suburbs can provide a safe and quiet environment, but they can also be lacking in community spirit. Smaller towns and rural areas can offer a sense of belonging, but they may not have the same amenities and opportunities as larger cities.

The key is to identify your priorities and find a place that aligns with your needs and lifestyle. Consider what kind of community you want to be a part of, what kind of social interactions you crave, and how you envision your life in a particular location. Ultimately, the best place to live is the one that feels right to you. Don't be afraid to explore different options and trust your intuition. Finding the right place to live is a journey, and it's worth taking.

For families, choosing the right location to live is a complex decision that goes beyond just finding a place to call home. It involves considering factors that directly impact the well-being and future of their children, primarily focusing on education and childcare options. This section will delve into the crucial aspects families need to consider when evaluating a location, ensuring that the chosen environment provides a nurturing and enriching foundation for their kids' growth.

Navigating the Education Landscape

The quality of education plays a pivotal role in shaping a child's future, and families naturally seek communities that offer exceptional learning opportunities. It's no longer enough to rely solely on a location's reputation; families must proactively research and understand the specifics of the school system.

Public vs. Private Schools: Understanding the distinction between public and private schools is crucial. Public schools are funded by the government and are free to attend, while private schools are privately financed and charge tuition. Public schools are subject to state and local regulations, while private schools have more autonomy. This difference translates into varying academic curricula, extracurricular activities, and overall learning environments.

Public Schools:

Advantages:

Free tuition, making them accessible to a broader range of families.

Typically offer diverse extracurricular activities like sports, clubs, and arts programs. Often have a more diverse student body, fostering an inclusive environment.

Disadvantages:

Can be overcrowded, impacting teacher-student ratios and

individual attention. May face funding constraints, limiting resources available for curriculum development and facilities.

Quality can vary significantly depending on the school district and local funding.

Private Schools:

Advantages:

Smaller class sizes, allowing for more individualized attention.

Often have advanced facilities and resources, enriching the learning experience. May offer specialized programs catering to specific interests or learning styles.

Disadvantages:

Significant tuition costs, making them less accessible to families with limited financial resources.

Can be more academically rigorous, potentially putting pressure on students.

May lack diversity, which can limit exposure to different cultures and perspectives.

School District Rankings and Performance: Relying solely on hearsay or anecdotal accounts isn't enough. Families need to delve into the data and objectively assess the school district's performance. Reputable organizations and websites provide valuable insights into school quality, allowing families to make informed decisions.

Key Data Points to Consider:

Test Scores: Standardized test scores (e.g., SAT, ACT) can indicate the academic performance of schools and districts. While not the sole measure of success, they offer a quantifiable benchmark.

Graduation Rates: High graduation rates indicate the school's ability to guide students to completion, a crucial indicator of academic success.

College Acceptance Rates: Understanding the percentage of graduates admitted to colleges and universities provides insight into the school's preparation for higher education.

Extracurricular Activities and Community Involvement: Beyond academic performance, consider the opportunities available for personal growth and development. Look for schools that actively promote extracurricular activities, fostering students' interests and talents. These may include:

Sports: From traditional team sports to individual athletic pursuits, schools should provide opportunities for students to develop their physical skills and teamwork.

Arts and Music: Involvement in music programs, drama, or visual arts enhances creativity and self-expression, enriching the student experience.

Clubs and Organizations: Encouraging participation in clubs and organizations fosters leadership skills, social connections, and community involvement.

School Safety and Security: A safe and secure learning environment is paramount for students' well-being. Investigate the school's safety measures, including:

Security Personnel: The presence of security personnel and trained staff ensures a proactive approach to safety.

Security Protocols: Understanding the school's safety protocols, such as lockdown procedures and visitor checks, provides reassurance.

Community Involvement: A collaborative effort between the school and the community promotes a shared sense of responsibility for student safety.

Teacher Quality and Experience: The quality of teachers directly influences the learning experience, shaping students' academic growth. Families should inquire about:

Teacher Qualifications: Are teachers certified and qualified in their subject areas?

Teacher Experience: Do teachers have adequate experience working with students?

Teacher Training: Do teachers receive ongoing professional development and training?

Parent Involvement and Communication: Strong communication between parents and schools is essential. Consider the following:

Parent-Teacher Communication: How readily accessible are teachers for communication and feedback?

Parent-Teacher Association (PTA): Is there an active PTA fostering parent involvement and collaboration with the school?

School Newsletters and Updates: Does the school provide regular updates to parents about events, curriculum, and student progress?

The Crucial Role of Childcare

While the focus often centers on education, childcare plays an equally crucial role, especially for families with younger children. Finding reliable and nurturing childcare arrangements is essential to provide a safe and stimulating environment while parents work.

Types of Childcare: Families have a range of options when it comes to childcare, each with its own advantages and disadvantages.

Family Daycare: This option involves caring for children in a home setting, often with a small group of children.

Advantages:

More intimate and personalized care, providing a warm and nurturing environment. Can be more affordable than other options.

Flexibility in scheduling.

Disadvantages:

Limited resources compared to larger centers. May lack structured learning activities.

Less regulated than larger facilities.

Childcare Centers: These facilities offer structured care for children, often with age-appropriate learning activities.

Advantages:

More regulated and monitored environment, ensuring safety and quality standards. Typically offer structured learning and play activities.

Larger staff-to-child ratios, providing more attention.

Disadvantages:

Can be more expensive than family daycare.

Less personalized care compared to smaller settings. Limited flexibility in scheduling.

Nannies: Hiring a nanny provides one-on-one care for children in the family's home.

Advantages:

Personalized care, providing a more individualized approach. Flexibility in scheduling and activities.

Disadvantages:

Can be expensive.

Requires careful vetting and background checks. May require more oversight and management.

Childcare Availability and Cost: Families need to research childcare options available in their chosen location and assess the cost. Consider the following:

Waitlists: Many popular childcare centers and daycare providers have long waitlists, so families must plan ahead.

Cost of Care: Childcare costs vary widely, depending on the type of facility, location, and age of the child.

Financial Assistance: Some states and communities offer financial assistance for families who qualify.

Quality and Licensing: Ensuring the quality and safety of childcare arrangements is paramount. Families must verify:

Licensing: Are all childcare providers properly licensed and in compliance with regulations?

Staff Qualifications: Do childcare providers have the necessary education and experience?

Child-to-Staff Ratios: Do staff-to-child ratios meet safety standards?

Safety and Hygiene: Does the facility meet safety and hygiene standards?

Childcare Scheduling and Flexibility: Families should consider their work schedules and childcare needs. Factors to consider include:

Hours of Operation: Do childcare providers operate during the hours needed by families?

Flexibility in Scheduling: Do providers offer flexibility in scheduling, accommodating late arrivals or early departures?

Balancing Education and Childcare Needs

For families with young children, choosing a location involves finding a balance between quality education and accessible, reliable childcare. It's about ensuring a holistic support system that nurtures children's growth and development while providing parents with peace of mind.

Proximity to Schools and Childcare Centers: Living close to schools and childcare centers simplifies logistics and reduces the burden of daily commutes.

Transportation Options: Evaluate transportation options available, including public transportation, walking paths, and cycling infrastructure.

Community Resources: Explore the availability of community resources that support families, such as playgroups, family centers, and community events.

Ultimately, finding the right location for a family with children requires a blend of research, planning, and careful consideration. It's a decision that shapes the family's future and ensures that children have the best possible start in life. By focusing on education, childcare, safety, and community, families can create a foundation for their children's growth and development, setting them up for success in all aspects of life.

Healthcare is a crucial aspect of life, and it's vital to consider the accessibility and quality of medical services when choosing a place to live. Moving to a new area without ensuring access to quality healthcare can be a risky decision. It's essential to understand the availability of medical professionals, hospitals, and clinics, as well as the overall healthcare system in the region.

For working individuals, access to healthcare becomes even more critical. If you have a chronic health condition or require regular medical attention, you need to ensure your new location offers adequate facilities and specialists. You might want to consider the proximity of your home to a reputable hospital or clinic and the availability of emergency medical services. Additionally, research the types of insurance plans accepted in the area and the cost of healthcare in general.

For retirees, healthcare becomes even more important, as they may have pre-existing conditions or need more frequent medical care. When choosing a location, retirees should prioritize areas with a strong network of medical professionals, hospitals, and clinics. It's essential to research the availability of specialists catering to specific health needs, such as geriatrics, cardiology, or oncology. Additionally, retirees should investigate the cost of healthcare in the area, including prescription drugs and long-term care facilities.

Families with young children need to consider the availability of pediatric care, including pediatricians, hospitals, and clinics. They should also consider the quality of childcare options and the ease of accessing essential healthcare services for children. Families should research the local school districts and their health and wellness programs. It's also important to consider the availability of emergency medical services for children.

When researching healthcare access and quality, you should consider the following factors:

Availability of Medical Professionals: Ensure that the area you're considering has a sufficient number of doctors, specialists, and other healthcare professionals to meet the needs of the community. You can find this information on websites like the American Medical Association's Physician Finder or the National Committee for Quality Assurance's (NCQA) Physician Finder.

Hospital and Clinic Quality: Look for hospitals and clinics that are accredited by organizations like the Joint Commission. Accreditation indicates that the facility meets certain quality standards. You can find this information on the Joint Commission's website. You should also look for hospitals and clinics with strong reputations for patient care and outcomes.

Healthcare System: Different states and countries have different healthcare systems. Some states have more robust public healthcare systems than others. It's essential to understand the healthcare system in the area you're considering, including the availability of public and private insurance options, the cost of healthcare, and the overall accessibility of medical care.

Emergency Medical Services: Check the availability of emergency medical services, including ambulances and emergency rooms, in the area you're considering. This information can be found on local government websites.

Prescription Drug Costs: Prescription drug costs can vary significantly depending on the location. You can use websites like GoodRx or the National Library of Medicine's MedlinePlus to compare prescription drug costs in different areas.

Access to Specialized Care: If you have a chronic health condition or require specialized care, ensure that the area you're considering has the necessary specialists and facilities. For example, if you have diabetes, you'll want to make sure there are endocrinologists and diabetes specialists available in the area.

In addition to these factors, consider the overall quality of life in the area. Does the area have good schools, parks, and recreational opportunities? Is there a strong sense of community? These factors can all contribute to your overall well-being and happiness.

Once you've considered all these factors, you can make an informed decision about where to live. Remember, choosing the right location is a significant decision. Take the time to research the options available and find the best fit for your needs and lifestyle.

How to Research Healthcare Access and Quality

There are various resources available to help you research healthcare access and quality in a specific location. Here are a few suggestions:

Websites: There are several websites that provide information on healthcare access and quality. These websites include:

Healthgrades: This website rates hospitals and physicians based on patient satisfaction, clinical outcomes, and other factors.

U.S. News & World Report: This website publishes an annual ranking of hospitals based on a variety of factors, including patient safety, efficiency, and effectiveness.

The Joint Commission: This website provides information on accredited hospitals and other healthcare organizations.

The Centers for Medicare & Medicaid Services (CMS): This website provides data on hospital quality, including readmission rates and patient satisfaction scores.

Local Organizations: You can also contact local organizations to get information on healthcare access and quality. These organizations include:

Local Chambers of Commerce: Chambers of Commerce often have information on healthcare providers in their area.

Local Health Departments: Health departments can

provide information on healthcare access and quality, as well as public health resources.

Patient Advocacy Groups: There are patient advocacy groups that can provide information on healthcare access and quality for specific conditions.

Word-of-Mouth: Talk to people who live in the area you're considering. They can provide valuable insights into the quality of healthcare in the area, including their experiences with local hospitals and physicians.

Case Studies

Here are a few case studies that illustrate the importance of considering healthcare access and quality when choosing a place to live.

Sarah, a young professional, moved to a new city for a job. She was excited about the opportunity but didn't consider the quality of healthcare in the area. After a few months, Sarah was diagnosed with a chronic condition. She struggled to find a doctor who could provide the specialized care she needed, and she was frustrated with the lack of access to quality medical services in the area. Sarah's story illustrates the importance of researching healthcare access and quality before moving to a new area. It can be a significant challenge to find adequate care once you've already relocated.

John, a retiree, moved to a small town in a rural area to be closer to his family. He assumed that the

healthcare in the area would be sufficient, but he quickly realized that access to specialized care was limited. John's story highlights the importance of considering healthcare access and quality when making a major relocation decision, particularly for retirees who may have pre-existing conditions or need more frequent medical care. John discovered that small towns may not have the same access to specialized healthcare as larger cities. It's essential to conduct thorough research to ensure that the healthcare facilities and specialists are available in the area.

Maria and her family moved to a new city for educational opportunities. They were pleased with the schools and the community, but were shocked by the lack of affordable childcare. They also found that access to quality pediatric care was limited. Maria's experience illustrates the importance of considering childcare options and pediatric care when choosing a location for families with young children. Families should consider the availability of quality childcare and pediatric services in the area. These factors are crucial for the well-being of their children.

Conclusion

Healthcare access and quality are critical factors to consider when choosing a place to live. It's vital to ensure that the area you choose has a strong healthcare system, adequate medical professionals, and quality hospitals and clinics. By considering these factors, you can make an informed decision that supports your health and well-being. Remember, your health is your most valuable asset. Take the time to research healthcare access and quality in your potential new home and make a choice that will keep you healthy and happy for years to come.

The quest to find the ideal location for a fulfilling life often involves a delicate dance between work opportunities and the lifestyle we envision. This balancing act can be particularly challenging for young professionals eager to establish their careers, retirees seeking a peaceful haven, and families striving to provide the best for their children.

Let's explore how to navigate this crucial decision-making process, considering factors such as career paths, work-life balance, and personal aspirations.

For young professionals, starting out in their careers, the temptation to chase high-paying jobs in bustling cities can be overwhelming. These urban centers often offer an array of exciting opportunities, a vibrant social scene, and a sense of belonging to a dynamic community. However, the allure of these metropolitan hotspots might come at a cost. The expenses associated with living in these cities can be substantial, including sky-high rents, expensive transportation, and a relentless pace of life that can leave little room for personal pursuits and relaxation.

Many young professionals find themselves caught in a cycle of working long hours to afford their high-cost lifestyle, leaving little time for personal growth, leisure activities, or exploring their passions. In this scenario, the balance between work and lifestyle can become skewed, leading to feelings of stress, burnout, and a sense of being constantly on the go.

To find a healthy equilibrium, young professionals might consider exploring alternative locations that offer a good blend of career opportunities, a more affordable cost of living, and a lifestyle that resonates with their values. Smaller cities and towns often provide a more relaxed environment, lower housing costs, and a greater sense of community. While career options might be more limited in these areas, opportunities for remote work or entrepreneurship are increasing rapidly. Imagine a young professional, Sarah, who had always dreamed of working in the tech industry in bustling San Francisco. She secured a well-paying job, but the cost of living was exorbitant, leaving her constantly worried about making ends meet. Sarah started feeling burnt out and found little time to pursue her passion for photography and travel. Realizing that her lifestyle was not sustainable, she decided to explore alternative options. She discovered a vibrant tech scene in Denver, Colorado, where she found a remote job that offered a better salary and a more affordable cost of living. Denver offered a diverse range of cultural experiences, outdoor adventures, and a more relaxed pace of life, allowing Sarah to balance her career with her passions and live a more fulfilling life.

For retirees seeking a peaceful and affordable haven, the search for the perfect location often focuses on factors like climate, healthcare, and community. Some retirees choose to downsize and relocate to smaller towns or rural areas, enjoying lower housing costs and a slower pace of life. Others opt for warmer climates to escape harsh winters and enjoy a more active lifestyle. While some retirees choose to stay in their current locations, others consider relocating abroad, drawn by the allure of lower living costs, rich cultures, and the opportunity to experience a different way of life.

Consider the story of John, a retired teacher who had always dreamed of living by the sea. He chose to downsize his home and move to a coastal town in Maine, where he could enjoy stunning ocean views, fresh seafood, and a close-knit community of retirees. John embraced the slower pace of life, spending his days walking along the beach, fishing, and volunteering at a local community center. While his income was reduced due to his retirement, his reduced expenses and the lower cost of living in Maine allowed him to live comfortably and pursue his passions.

Families, on the other hand, often prioritize factors like safety, education, and access to childcare when choosing a location. Finding a place that provides a safe and nurturing environment for children, access to quality education, and affordable childcare options is paramount. While big cities might offer some of these amenities, families often find that suburban areas provide a better balance of affordability, safety, and educational opportunities.

Imagine the Smith family, who were looking for a place to raise their two young children. They decided to relocate from the city to a suburb with a good school system and plenty of green spaces for their children to play. They found a house with a backyard and a community with a strong sense of family. The family was able to find affordable childcare options nearby and enjoyed the quieter pace of life, allowing them to spend quality time together as a family.

Finding the right balance between work opportunities and lifestyle is an ongoing process, constantly evolving as our priorities and circumstances change. It's crucial to regularly reassess our needs and aspirations, considering factors such as career goals, financial situations, and personal values.

Here are some key questions to guide your decision-making process:

What are your non-negotiable lifestyle preferences? (e.g., climate, access to nature, community values, cultural amenities)

What are your career goals, and how flexible are you with location? How important is affordability in your decision-making?

What are your priorities for raising a family (if applicable)? Are you willing to consider relocating abroad?

By answering these questions honestly, you can gain a clearer understanding of your priorities and start exploring locations that align with your vision for a fulfilling and balanced life.

Remember, there is no one-size-fits-all solution. Finding the ideal location is a personal journey that requires careful consideration, exploration, and a willingness to adapt as your life evolves. Embrace the process, be open to possibilities, and trust your instincts. The perfect place is out there, waiting to be discovered.

As the U.S. faces a changing political landscape, many families are reexamining their priorities when relocating or picking a new place to live. Concerns about education, safety and health care are driving these decisions as parents seek communities that address the unique needs and challenges facing their families.

To determine the best states for raising a family in 2025, ConsumerAffairs compared each state on cost, safety, education, health care and quality of life. For a deeper look at how these rankings were determined, see our full methodology below.

The Best States To Raise A Family in 2024-2025

The top five states for raising a family are Vermont, Maine, Pennsylvania, New Hampshire and Wyoming.

1. Vermont

Vermont earned its spot as one of the top states to raise a family in by ranking first in quality of life and ranking high in child health care, education and safety. The state has the highest number of libraries per capita in the nation, with 25 libraries per 100,000 residents.

Vermont is also home to the second-highest number of national and state parks per capita (8.5 per 100,000 residents), providing plenty of outdoor recreational opportunities for families. Vermont also stands out for its air quality, ranking third. As Trevor Summerfield, director of advocacy for the

American Lung Association in Vermont, put it, "Vermont continues to be one of the best places to live when it comes to (common) pollutants" due to its low levels of harmful air pollution.

The state ranks sixth for pediatric health care access and for public education. In addition, Vermont's low violent crime rate, the sixth lowest in the nation, further solidifies its reputation as a safe and family-friendly place to live.

2. Maine

Maine stands out as a top contender for families, with high rankings in quality of life and safety. It has the lowest overall violent crime rate, making it a top destination for parents most concerned with safety. Maine's draw for families is further highlighted by its third-place ranking for overall quality of life, including having (along with Wyoming) the lowest percentage of children living in poverty, at just 5%.

Families in Maine benefit from the state's natural beauty and many outdoor activities. It is home to Acadia National Park, known for its scenic coastal views and family-friendly hiking trails.

3. Pennsylvania

Pennsylvania ranks highly for raising a family due to impressive scores in public education, safety and pediatric health care. It is fifth in public education, with the second-highest public high school graduation rate in the country, at 96%. Additionally, Pennsylvania ranks in the top 10 for the number of pediatricians per 100,000 children (147), providing children in the state with adequate access to medical care.

Gov. Josh Shapiro's 2024-25 budget for Pennsylvania includes $1.11 billion in additional funding for K-12 public education, focusing on equitable distribution and special education enhancements. These investments reflect the state's ongoing efforts to improve its education system — an important factor for parents and guardians seeking a supportive environment for their children.

4. New Hampshire

New Hampshire ranks as a top choice for families because of its blend of low crime rates, excellent quality of life and accessible health care. The state is second in air quality, and it ranks third for the number of national and state parks, at close to seven per 100,000 people. Additionally, New Hampshire places in the top five for public libraries, with 16 per 100,000 residents.

These community resources complement the state's strong health care system. New Hampshire has the second-lowest infant mortality rate in the U.S. at 3.5 per 1,000 live births. With 76% of children regularly receiving preventive medical and dental care, and nearly 98% of children having health insurance coverage, New Hampshire has a robust system for supporting children's health care.

New Hampshire is also the safest state in the nation, with the third-lowest violent crime rate and the lowest property crime rate in the U.S.

5. Wyoming

One of Wyoming's biggest draws is its affordability. It ranked as the seventh-most affordable state, offering a great cost of living for families. Child care costs average $8,737 annually, which is the lowest among any state in the top five.

Additionally, Wyoming excels in safety, ranking in the top 10, and has a high 94% high school graduation rate, ninth highest in the U.S. The state also places high for the fewest children living in poverty, at just 5%, and is in the top 10 for air quality.

However, Wyoming's health care system faces challenges, ranking near the bottom of all states. Around 14% of families struggle to afford their children's medical care, and only 91% of children are covered by insurance.

Despite these health care limitations, Wyoming remains a top choice for families seeking a slower pace at an affordable price.

Which states ranked poorly for raising a family?

The bottom five states for raising a family are all located in the West and South and face significant challenges in education and quality of life.

California ranks at the bottom, struggling with high child poverty rates, a shortage of libraries and bad air quality.

Texas follows closely behind, scoring poorly in health care, safety and quality of life. The state has the lowest pediatric health care score, with the highest percentages of uninsured children and families that can't afford their children's health care bills.

New Mexico, Arizona and Nevada round out the bottom, with poor public education and lower rankings in quality of life.

Washington, D.C., across five categories — affordability, safety, education, pediatric health care and quality of life — to determine overall rankings for raising a family in 2025.

However, depending on your family's unique needs, some aspects, like health care or cost of living, may carry more weight. By taking a deeper look at all of these factors, you can determine which state is right for your family.

How to pick the best place for your family

Choosing the best place to raise your family means considering general quality of life factors as well as aspects that affect your child's development. Sheel Jagani, the director of special populations integration at the Texas Education Agency, which oversees primary and secondary education in the state, shared her insights on what parents should consider when evaluating potential new communities.

- **Evaluate hidden costs of living.** Beyond housing costs, consider regional price differences for essentials like food, clothing and child care, which can vary widely. Expenses like heating in colder states or insurance premiums in disaster-prone areas may also add up, affecting overall affordability.

- **Prioritize community resources.** Seek out communities with active support systems, such as recreation centers, libraries with children's programming and parent groups. These resources help families integrate quickly and offer a sense of belonging, particularly if you're moving without an established support network. "Community centers like libraries and parks can be central to supplementing what's available in a school and ensure kids have access to enrichment and play," Jagani said.
- **Consider school quality and extracurriculars.** Research local schools and extracurricular programs to understand the educational opportunities available. Schools that offer enrichment programs, sports and arts activities provide an additional layer of support for children's personal and academic growth. "Outside of academics, you may want to find out if the transportation options, nutrition options, after-school programs and facilities meet the needs of your family," Jagani said.
- **Look into state-specific policies.** Certain states have policies or programs designed to benefit families with school-age children. Whether it's funding for charter schools, after-school care programs or state-funded college savings accounts, these can make a big difference in your family's quality of life.

To determine the best states in which to raise a family in 2025, the ConsumerAffairs Research Team compared all 50 U.S.

states and Washington, D.C., across five weighted categories worth a total of 100 points:

- **Affordability (30 points):** The affordability score is based on the annual cost of raising a child in each state, covering expenses like food, rent, child care and tax credits. Data sources include the U.S. Census Bureau, Child Care Aware of America and the National Conference of State Legislatures.
- **Safety (20 points):** The safety score is based on five metrics: violent crime, property crime, driving safety, public safety and climate safety, using data from ConsumerAffairs' study on the safest states in America.
- **Education (20 points):** The education score is based on four categories: K-12 performance, school funding and resources, higher education quality and school safety, using data from ConsumerAffairs' study on the best states for public education.
- **Pediatric health care (20 points):** The pediatric health care score considers five metrics: pediatricians per 100,000 people up to age 21, infant mortality rate, percentage of uninsured children, percentage of children who did not receive preventive care and percentage of families struggling with medical bills. Data sources include America's Health Rankings, the Centers for Disease Control and Prevention and the Child and Adolescent Health Measurement Initiative.
- **Quality of life (10 points):** The quality of life score is based on four metrics: percentage of children

in poverty, number of state and national parks per 100,000 people, number of public libraries per 100,000 people and ConsumerAffairs' analysis of data on cities with the best air quality. Data sources include the Annie E. Casey Foundation, Outside Interactive, the National Association of State Park Directors and the National Center for Education Statistics.

TOP 5 BEST STATES TO RETIRE IN

Finding the right mix of cost, care and community.

Retirement is the perfect time to reimagine where and how you want to live. With 50 states to choose from, selecting the right retirement destination can feel overwhelming. But when you prioritize the essentials – tax benefits, health care access, cost of living and community and lifestyle – a few standout states emerge as ideal choices.

To help you consider this important decision, we've rounded up the top five best states to retire in for 2025, based on these critical factors.

1. FLORIDA

Florida has long been considered a retirement haven and for good reason. Its tax-friendly policies, excellent health care options and vibrant lifestyle make it a top choice for retirees across the United States. Whether you're looking to maximize your savings or enjoy endless sunshine, Florida offers something for everyone.

TAX BENEFITS

Florida is one of the few states with no state income tax, allowing retirees to retain more of their Social Security benefits, pension payments and other retirement income. There are also no estate or inheritance taxes, making wealth transfer to family members more straightforward. Additionally, seniors can benefit from homestead exemptions, which reduce property taxes and lower annual housing costs significantly.

HEALTH CARE ACCESS

Florida excels in health care, offering top-tier medical facilities specializing in geriatrics and senior care. It also has a high concentration of providers and specialists catering to retirees, helping ensure easy access to services.

COST OF LIVING

While housing prices in popular cities like Miami can be higher, many parts of Florida provide affordable housing options below the national average. From cozy condos to spacious suburban homes, there's something to fit virtually every budget.

COMMUNITY AND LIFESTYLE

Florida offers retirees a vibrant lifestyle with endless recreational activities, from golf courses to sandy beaches. Seniors can also choose from a range of retirement communities where they can stay active and socially engaged.

2. ARIZONA

Known for its breathtaking landscapes and warm climate, Arizona is a fantastic retirement destination. It offers retirees a balance of affordability, tax advantages and opportunities for an active lifestyle.

TAX BENEFITS

Arizona has no tax on Social Security benefits, helping ensure your fixed income goes further – plus, they have reasonable property taxes and some deductions are available for certain retirement income.

HEALTH CARE ACCESS

Arizona has a robust health care system, anchored by renowned facilities such as the Mayo Clinic in Phoenix. Retirees benefit from specialized geriatric care and wellness programs, and accessible health care services in both urban centers and smaller communities.

COST OF LIVING

Ranked as the third most affordable state, Arizona is an excellent option for retirees seeking a reasonable cost of living, offering plenty of options for those on a fixed income.

COMMUNITY AND LIFESTYLE

Arizona is perfect for those who love outdoor adventures and cultural experiences. Whether it's stunning hiking trails and golf courses or vibrant arts scenes, Arizona has a welcoming community atmosphere with plenty to do.

3. TENNESSEE

Tennessee combines low living costs with a rich cultural heritage, making it an attractive option for retirees. From the music-filled streets of Nashville to the scenic beauty of the Great Smoky Mountains, this state has it all.

TAX BENEFITS

Tennessee's tax structure is among the most retiree-friendly in the country. There's no state income tax, so your Social Security benefits and retirement income will be untouched, and low property taxes can help you stretch your savings even further.

HEALTH CARE ACCESS

Facilities in Tennessee's major cities, like Nashville and Chattanooga, are well-regarded for their care for older adults.

COST OF LIVING

Tennessee has one of the lowest costs of living in the United States, at 10% below the national average. Everyday expenses such as utilities and groceries are budget-friendly, and housing is affordable, with options ranging from suburban homes to retirement communities priced below the national average.

COMMUNITY AND LIFESTYLE

Retirees will find plenty to love about Tennessee, from the rich cultural scene, especially in cities like Memphis and Nashville, to the many outdoor activities in the mountains and along the Mississippi River.

4. DELAWARE

Delaware may be small in size, but it offers big advantages for retirees. With its favorable tax policies, serene environment and proximity to major metropolitan areas, Delaware is a hidden gem for those looking to enjoy their golden years.

TAX BENEFITS

Delaware is consistently ranked as one of the most tax-friendly states for retirees, thanks to:

- No state or local sales tax, saving you money on everyday purchases.
- Tax exemptions that allow residents over 60 to exclude up to $12,500 of investment and qualified pension income, including out-of-state government pensions, from state taxes.No estate or inheritance taxes, ensuring you can leave a legacy without additional state tax burdens.

HEALTH CARE ACCESS

Delaware is home to many respected healthcare providers, which can offer easy access to comprehensive, high-quality care for both routine and specialized health needs.

COST OF LIVING

While Delaware's cost of living can vary, its smaller towns and communities often provide affordable housing options.

Retirees can enjoy suburban charm without sacrificing financial security.

COMMUNITY AND LIFESTYLE

Delaware offers a relaxed and peaceful environment with charming coastal towns perfect for enjoying a quieter lifestyle. At the same time, residents get easy access to urban amenities in nearby Philadelphia and Baltimore.

5. SOUTH CAROLINA

South Carolina's scenic coastlines, historic towns and friendly communities make it a standout for retirees. Whether you're looking for tranquility or a lively cultural scene, this state delivers.

TAX BENEFITS

South Carolina offers significant tax advantages. Not only is there no tax on Social Security income, ensuring more of your benefits can stay in your bank account, but the state also offers deductions on other retirement income and low property taxes.

HEALTH CARE ACCESS

There are well-equipped hospitals and senior care facilities throughout the state, and South Carolina is continuing to expand its health care infrastructure to cater to its growing senior population.

COST OF LIVING

With a cost of living of 6% below the national average, South Carolina is one of the most affordable states for retirees: Housing costs are particularly appealing, with a range of affordable options in cities like Charleston and Greenville.

COMMUNITY AND LIFESTYLE

South Carolina combines natural beauty with rich history. Coastal towns like Myrtle Beach offer relaxation and recreation, while historic Charleston provides a cultural haven with vibrant arts and dining scenes.

PLANNING FOR A SECURE, FULFILLING RETIREMENT

Choosing the best state to retire in is about balancing financial priorities with your personal aspirations. The states listed here – Florida, Arizona, Tennessee, Delaware and South Carolina – excel in tax benefits, health care access, cost of living, and community and lifestyle, offering the benefits you need to help make the most of your retirement years. In weighing potential options for retirement living, the benefits we've outlined here make these five states great candidates for your consideration.

5

LIVING ABROAD: OPPORTUNITIES AND CHALLENGES

A Lifestyle Of A Globe Trotter

The allure of escaping the high cost of living in the United States has been a recurring theme throughout history, drawing people to seek greener pastures abroad. This yearning for a more affordable life, coupled with the desire to experience different cultures, has led many individuals and families to embark on adventures in countries that offer a lower cost of living and a high quality of life. While the allure of a lower cost of living abroad is undeniable, it's crucial to understand that it's not a one-size-fits-all solution.

Navigating the World of Affordable Living

Before diving into specific countries, it's essential to establish a framework for evaluating these destinations. Here's a checklist of factors to consider when exploring countries with a lower cost of living:

Cost of Living Index: This index compares the prices of essential goods and services like food, transportation, housing, and utilities in different cities worldwide. It helps you understand the relative affordability of various locations compared to your current city.

Currency Exchange Rates: Fluctuating exchange rates can significantly impact the cost of living, so it's crucial to monitor them closely. A favorable exchange rate can make your budget stretch further, while an unfavorable rate can diminish your purchasing power.

Housing Costs: Rent and property prices vary greatly across countries, so researching typical housing costs is essential. Keep in mind that even if the overall cost of living is lower, rent or property prices in major cities or popular tourist destinations may be higher.

Healthcare and Insurance: Understanding healthcare systems and insurance needs in foreign countries is essential. You'll want to know if the country has universal healthcare, if you'll need private insurance, and what the costs might be.

Visa Requirements: Researching visa regulations is a vital step. Depending on your nationality and your reason for living abroad, you may need to apply for a specific visa or residency permit.

Cultural Adaptability: Living in a foreign country requires a willingness to adapt to new customs, traditions, and language. Be prepared to embrace the cultural differences and learn the local language, even if it's just basic phrases.

Job Market: If you're planning to work abroad, consider the job market and employment opportunities in your desired country. Researching industries, salary ranges, and visa requirements for employment is crucial.

A World of Possibilities

With these factors in mind, let's explore some countries that consistently rank high for their affordability and quality of life:

Southeast Asia: A Tapestry of Affordability and Culture

Southeast Asia, with its stunning landscapes, rich history, and vibrant cultures, has become a popular destination for digital nomads, retirees, and families seeking a more affordable lifestyle.

Thailand: Known for its friendly people, delicious cuisine, and beautiful beaches, Thailand offers a lower cost of living compared to many Western countries. You can live comfortably in Thailand on a relatively modest budget, especially outside of major tourist hubs.

Vietnam: Vietnam's captivating natural beauty, bustling cities, and mouthwatering cuisine have made it a sought-after destination for expats. From the ancient temples of Hue to the vibrant streets of Ho Chi Minh City, Vietnam offers a diverse range of experiences at a fraction of the cost of many Western nations.

Malaysia: This multicultural nation offers a blend of modern amenities and traditional charm. With its strategic location in Southeast Asia, Malaysia offers a gateway to exploring the region while enjoying a lower cost of living and a relatively high quality of life.

South America: A Land of Diversity and Affordability

South America, with its captivating natural wonders, rich cultural heritage, and vibrant cities, offers an enticing mix of adventure and affordability.

Ecuador: Ecuador is a haven for nature lovers, with its stunning Andes Mountains, Amazon rainforest, and Galapagos Islands. The cost of living in Ecuador is generally lower than in many other South American countries, making it an attractive destination for expats seeking a budget-friendly lifestyle.

Colombia: Colombia has undergone a significant transformation in recent years, emerging as a safe and welcoming destination for expats. With its charming colonial cities, breathtaking landscapes, and lively cultural scene, Colombia offers an appealing mix of affordability and adventure.

Argentina: Argentina, known for its tango, vibrant culture, and stunning natural beauty, has become a popular destination for digital nomads and retirees. The cost of living in Argentina is generally lower than in many other countries, making it a budget-friendly option for those seeking a vibrant lifestyle.

Eastern Europe: Where History Meets Affordability

Eastern Europe, with its fascinating history, rich culture, and stunning architecture, offers a unique blend of affordability and cultural immersion.

Portugal: Portugal has become a popular destination for digital nomads and retirees, offering a lower cost of living, a pleasant climate, and a rich cultural heritage. Its charming towns, beautiful beaches, and delicious cuisine have made Portugal a sought-after destination.

Czech Republic: The Czech Republic, with its captivating cities like Prague and Brno, offers a blend of affordability and

European charm. The country's rich history, vibrant culture, and stunning architecture attract visitors from around the world.

Poland: Poland has experienced significant economic growth in recent years, making it an increasingly attractive destination for expats. The country's vibrant cities, rich history, and affordable lifestyle offer a compelling combination for those seeking a new adventure.

The Importance of Research and Personalization

While this list provides a starting point, it's crucial to conduct thorough research tailored to your specific needs and preferences.

Consider your lifestyle: Are you a city dweller or a nature enthusiast? Are you seeking a vibrant nightlife or a peaceful retreat? Your lifestyle choices will heavily influence the best destinations for you.

Think about your finances: What's your budget? How long do you plan to live abroad? Your financial situation will dictate your choices and help you narrow down the most suitable countries.

Research healthcare systems: Understand the healthcare systems and insurance needs in your potential destinations.

Learn about visa requirements: Ensure you meet the necessary visa or residency permit requirements.

Connect with other expats: Reach out to other expats who have already made the transition to get insights and firsthand experiences.

Embracing the Journey: A Life Beyond the Familiar

Living abroad is a journey filled with both challenges and rewards.

Be prepared for cultural differences: Expect to encounter cultural differences, from language barriers to social norms. Embrace these differences as opportunities for growth and understanding.

Develop a strong support network: Building a support network of other expats or local friends can make your transition smoother.

Learn the language: Even a basic understanding of the local language can significantly improve your experience.

Stay adaptable and open-minded: Be willing to adapt to new situations and embrace the unexpected.

Celebrate the small victories: Living abroad is a continuous learning experience. Celebrate your achievements and savor the moments that make the journey worthwhile.

Beyond the Cost of Living: Finding Your True Home

The decision to live abroad is not just about finding a lower cost of living. It's about seeking a new experience, embracing new cultures, and discovering a deeper sense of self. While financial considerations are important, it's equally crucial to consider your personal values and your desire for adventure and growth.

Remember, there's no one-size-fits-all answer. The best place to live is the one that aligns with your needs, aspirations, and personal preferences. By carefully researching, planning, and embracing the journey, you can unlock a world of possibilities and create a life that's both fulfilling and financially secure.

Moving to a new country, especially one with a different culture and language, can be an exhilarating and daunting experience. It's an adventure into the unknown, a chance to broaden your horizons, immerse yourself in a new way of life, and forge connections with people from diverse backgrounds. However, the transition can be challenging, requiring adaptability, resilience, and a willingness to embrace the unfamiliar. Cultural differences, language barriers, and the sheer magnitude of adapting to a new environment can present hurdles that need to be navigated with care.

Navigating cultural differences is a key aspect of living abroad. Every culture has its own set of norms, values, and beliefs, shaping its social interactions, communication styles, and even the way people perceive the world. While some cultural differences may seem subtle or even amusing, others can be significant and potentially impact your daily life. For instance, in some cultures, direct eye contact is considered respectful, while in others, it can be perceived as aggressive or confrontational.

Understanding these nuances is crucial to avoid misunderstandings and build meaningful relationships.

Language barriers can be a major obstacle, particularly if you don't speak the native tongue. While some countries have large English-speaking communities, many others do not, making daily communication a challenge. From ordering food to attending meetings, basic interactions can feel daunting. The inability to communicate effectively can lead to feelings of isolation, frustration, and even a sense of helplessness. However, it's important to remember that language is not just about words; it's also about cultural understanding. Even if you don't speak the language fluently, being open to learning and engaging with the local culture can bridge communication gaps.

Cultural Adaptation and Language Learning Strategies

Embrace Humility and Open-mindedness: The most crucial element of successful cultural adaptation is recognizing that your own culture is not inherently superior to another. Be open to learning from different perspectives, understanding that cultural differences are not necessarily right or wrong but simply different. This attitude allows you to approach unfamiliar situations with curiosity rather than judgment. Research and Preparation: Before you move, take the time to learn about the customs, traditions, and social norms of your new home. Familiarize yourself with the country's history, its political landscape, and its values. Understanding the cultural context will help you navigate social situations more effectively and avoid potential faux pas.

Language Learning: A Continuous Journey: The sooner you begin learning the local language, the better. While basic phrases can be useful, becoming fluent requires time, dedication, and immersion. Even if your language skills are initially limited, don't be afraid to try. The local people will likely appreciate your effort.

Seek Out Local Connections: One of the best ways to learn about a culture is to interact with its people. Connect with locals through social events, cultural activities, or even casual conversations. Ask questions, share your experiences, and actively listen to their insights. Forming friendships with locals can not only enrich your cultural experience but also provide invaluable support and guidance as you adjust to life in your new country.

Join Expatriate Communities: While it's important to connect with locals, connecting with fellow expats can also be helpful. They can offer valuable advice, share their experiences, and provide a sense of community during the initial adjustment period. Stay Engaged in Your Own Culture: While immersing yourself in a new culture is vital, it's equally important to maintain connections to your own cultural heritage. Stay in touch with family and friends back home, participate in cultural events, and nurture the aspects of your own culture that you value.

Find Your Community: Whether it's through a shared hobby, a local interest group, or a volunteer organization, finding a community where you feel comfortable and connected is essential for well-being. Shared interests and activities can create a sense of belonging and alleviate feelings of isolation.

Navigating Cultural Differences: A Case Study

Let's imagine Sarah, a young professional from the United States, moves to Tokyo, Japan, to pursue a career in technology. Sarah, accustomed to a fast-paced, direct communication style, is initially thrown off by the Japanese culture's emphasis on harmony and indirect communication. She finds herself struggling to understand the nuances of non-verbal cues, like bowing and using polite language. She also encounters difficulty expressing disagreement or voicing her opinions directly, as these actions are often seen as confrontational.

However, Sarah, being open-minded and eager to learn, starts taking Japanese language classes and attending cultural events. She makes an effort to understand the cultural context behind Japanese communication, learning about the value of harmony and the importance of avoiding conflict. She also observes the behavior of her Japanese colleagues, trying to decipher the subtle cues they use in their interactions. Slowly but surely, she begins to adapt to the cultural nuances, becoming more comfortable with the Japanese communication style.

Through her immersion in Japanese culture, Sarah learns to appreciate the value of indirect communication, recognizing its effectiveness in building relationships and maintaining harmony. She discovers that a more nuanced approach, focusing on building consensus and fostering mutual understanding, can be just as effective as a direct communication style.

Language Learning: A Journey of Discovery

Language learning is a transformative experience that goes beyond acquiring vocabulary and grammar. It's a journey of discovery that unlocks a deeper understanding of a culture's history, values, and worldview. When you learn a new language, you're not just acquiring new words; you're gaining access to a whole new way of thinking and interacting with the world.

For instance, let's consider the Arabic language. Beyond its beautiful script and intricate grammar, the Arabic language is steeped in history and culture. Learning Arabic involves delving into a world of poetry, philosophy, and literature that has shaped civilizations for centuries. The language itself reflects the values of the Arab culture, emphasizing eloquence, precision, and a deep appreciation for language as an art form.

Learning a new language is also an opportunity to challenge your own perspectives and broaden your understanding of the world. When you learn a new language, you're forced to step outside of your own cultural bubble and see the world from a different angle. This can lead to greater empathy, cultural sensitivity, and a deeper appreciation for the diversity of human thought.

Strategies for Overcoming Language Barriers

Immersion: The Fastest Way to Learn: The best way to learn a new language is to immerse yourself in it. Surround yourself with the language as much as possible, whether it's through television, music, books, or daily interactions.

Find a Language Partner: Having a language partner can accelerate your learning progress. It provides a safe space to practice speaking and listening, receive feedback, and learn from each other's cultural perspectives.

Utilize Technology: Apps and Online Resources: Several language learning apps and online resources can enhance your language learning experience. These platforms offer interactive exercises, games, and personalized lessons to make learning engaging and effective.

Embrace Mistakes and Be Patient: Language learning is a process, and it takes time. Be patient with yourself, and don't be afraid to make mistakes. Every mistake is an opportunity to learn and grow.

Don't be Afraid to Ask for Help: Don't hesitate to ask locals for help when you're struggling with language barriers. Most people are willing to help, and even if they don't speak English fluently, they can often use gestures and facial expressions to communicate.

Beyond Language: Cultural Sensitivity and Understanding

While language is an important tool for communication, it's not the only way to connect with people from different cultures. Nonverbal communication, such as body language, facial expressions, and gestures, can be just as powerful as spoken words.

Understanding cultural nuances in nonverbal communication can help you navigate social situations more effectively and avoid misunderstandings.

For instance, in some cultures, a firm handshake is a common greeting, while in others, a light bow or a wave might be more appropriate. Similarly, the amount of personal space considered comfortable varies significantly across cultures. Being aware of these differences can help you avoid making people feel uncomfortable or offended.

Living abroad is a transformative journey, full of challenges and rewards. It's a chance to step outside of your comfort zone, experience a new way of life, and broaden your horizons. By embracing cultural differences, learning the local language, and engaging with the local community, you can make the most of this incredible opportunity and create lasting memories that will enrich your life.

The decision to live abroad is a thrilling and complex one, filled with exciting possibilities and potential challenges. While the allure of a lower cost of living, diverse cultures, and new experiences is enticing, it's crucial to understand the legal and financial implications that come with this life-altering choice.

Navigating the Legal Maze

Before packing your bags, it's essential to understand the legal framework of your chosen country. Each nation has its own set of rules regarding residency, work permits, and citizenship. For example, obtaining a visa to live and work in a foreign country can be a long and bureaucratic process, requiring extensive paperwork, background checks, and potentially language proficiency tests.

The Visa Landscape

The type of visa you need depends on your purpose for living abroad. Some common visa categories include:

Tourist Visa: For short-term stays, allowing you to explore the country as a visitor.

Work Visa: Permits you to work in the country, often requiring a job offer from a local employer.

Student Visa: Allows you to study in the country, requiring enrollment in an accredited educational institution.

Retirement Visa: Specifically designed for individuals seeking to retire in the country, often with age and financial requirements.

The Path to Citizenship

Many countries offer pathways to citizenship, often involving residency requirements and language proficiency tests.

However, these processes can be lengthy and demanding, often requiring years of residency before eligibility for citizenship.

Financial Preparations

Living abroad presents unique financial considerations that require careful planning. Understanding these aspects early on can significantly reduce stress and ensure a smoother transition.

Opening Bank Accounts

You'll need to establish local bank accounts to manage your finances in your new home. Research local banks and their services, including currency exchange rates and fees. Opening an account may require providing documentation like a passport, visa, and proof of address.

Currency Conversion

Be prepared for fluctuations in exchange rates. While some countries have stable currencies, others experience significant fluctuations. Consider using a reputable currency exchange service and budgeting for potential losses in currency conversion.

Taxes and Financial Reporting

Tax regulations vary greatly from country to country. It's crucial to understand your tax obligations in both your home country and the country where you're living. You may need to file tax returns in both countries, and failure to comply with tax rules could result in penalties.

Estate Planning and Inheritance

If you own property or have assets in your home country, you'll need to update your estate planning documents to reflect your new residency status. This may involve creating or revising wills, trusts, and powers of attorney to ensure that your assets are distributed according to your wishes.

Healthcare Considerations

Healthcare systems and insurance coverage differ significantly from country to country. Research the healthcare system in your new home and assess your healthcare needs. You may need to purchase additional health insurance or explore options like private healthcare.

Safety and Security

Before moving abroad, research the safety and security of your chosen destination. Understanding crime rates, political stability, and emergency response procedures is crucial for your personal safety.

Adapting to New Cultures and Customs

Living in a new culture can be both exciting and challenging. Embrace the opportunity to learn about local customs, traditions, and etiquette. Being respectful of local norms will help you build connections and feel more integrated into your new community.

Language Barriers

The ability to communicate effectively is essential for navigating daily life in a new country. If you're not fluent in the local language, consider learning basic phrases or enrolling in language classes. This will help you interact with people, access services, and immerse yourself in your new environment.

Navigating the Transition

Moving abroad is a major life transition. Allow yourself time to adjust to your new surroundings, embrace the culture, and build a new support system. Connect with other expats, explore local activities, and find ways to stay connected with your friends and family back home.

Embracing the Adventure

Living abroad is a remarkable journey that can offer profound personal growth and a fresh perspective on life. By carefully planning and addressing the legal and financial considerations, you can navigate the challenges and fully embrace the opportunities that await you in your new home. Remember, the key to a successful transition lies in preparation, research, and a willingness to embrace the unknown.

Stepping into a new country is like embarking on a captivating adventure, a journey filled with unknown landscapes and unfamiliar customs. While the allure of lower living costs in foreign lands can be tempting, it's crucial to address a critical aspect of this adventure: healthcare and insurance. Navigating healthcare systems and insurance policies in a foreign country can be a complex labyrinth, requiring careful planning and understanding.

Let's imagine you're a young professional, perhaps a software engineer, seeking a change of scenery. You've set your sights on a vibrant city like Lisbon, Portugal, known for its rich history, beautiful beaches, and a relatively low cost of living. While the prospect of exploring charming cobblestone streets and indulging in delicious pastel de nata pastries is exciting, the reality is that you'll need to ensure your health and well-being are protected in this new environment.

Healthcare Systems: A World of Differences

First, it's essential to understand that healthcare systems vary significantly from country to country. The United States, with its private insurance-driven system, contrasts sharply with universal healthcare systems like those in Canada and most European countries. In Portugal, you'll encounter a public healthcare system known as the Serviço Nacional de Saúde (SNS), a government-funded system providing essential medical care.

While the SNS covers basic services like doctor visits, hospital stays, and emergency care, it may not cover all treatments or procedures. The level of coverage and waiting times for non-emergency services can vary. For instance, if you require specialized medical care, you might face longer waiting times within the public system. This is where private health insurance comes into play.

The Role of Private Health Insurance

Private health insurance in Portugal, like in many other countries, offers greater flexibility and faster access to care. It can cover a wider range of medical services, including specialized treatments and procedures, often with shorter waiting times. You can choose from various private insurance plans based on your needs and budget.

However, keep in mind that private insurance can be expensive, especially if you require comprehensive coverage. Before you commit to a plan, it's essential to carefully evaluate your medical needs and compare different insurance providers and policies.

Insurance Options for Expats

As an expat, you have several insurance options:

International Health Insurance: International health insurance plans are designed specifically for people living or traveling abroad. They offer comprehensive coverage, including medical expenses, emergency medical evacuation, and repatriation.

Local Health Insurance: You can also opt for local health insurance in Portugal, which typically provides coverage within the country. However, local plans may not offer the same level of coverage as international plans, especially for emergency situations or medical evacuation.

Travel Insurance: Travel insurance is essential for short-term trips abroad. It provides coverage for medical expenses, trip cancellations, and other unforeseen circumstances. If you're planning a long-term stay, travel insurance might not be sufficient as it typically has a limited duration.

Considerations for Choosing an Insurance Plan

When selecting an insurance plan, several key factors come into play: Coverage: Assess the specific coverage offered by each plan, including medical expenses, emergency evacuation, repatriation, and other benefits.

Premiums: Compare the monthly premiums of different plans to find one that fits your budget.

Exclusions: Pay close attention to any exclusions or limitations in the policy, such as pre-existing conditions or specific treatments.

Claims Process: Understand the process for filing claims and any associated fees or requirements.

Network: If you choose a private health insurance plan, check the network of healthcare providers to ensure access to qualified doctors and hospitals.

Language Support: If you're not fluent in the local language, choose a plan that provides language support for claims and customer service.

Navigating the Healthcare System

Once you have your insurance in place, you'll need to understand how to access healthcare in your new home.

Finding a Doctor: You can find doctors through recommendations from expats or local residents, online directories, or your insurance provider's network.

Appointments: Appointments may require pre-booking, and you'll need to confirm the doctor's acceptance of your insurance plan.

Communication: If you have limited language skills, consider seeking out doctors who speak English or bringing a translator to appointments.

Prescription Medications: Ensure you have a valid prescription and understand how to obtain medications in your new country.

Emergency Care: If you need emergency care, contact your insurance provider for guidance and access to the nearest hospital or clinic.

Embracing the Healthcare Journey

Adapting to a new healthcare system can be challenging, but it's also an opportunity to learn and grow. Take the time to understand the system in your new home and seek support from fellow expats, local residents, and your insurance provider.

Remember, your health is your most valuable asset. By taking proactive steps to understand and protect your healthcare needs, you can embrace the adventure of living abroad with peace of mind. And as you navigate this new world of medical care, don't forget to savor the cultural experiences and culinary delights your new home offers.

The world is vast, and for many, the allure of a new culture, a slower pace of life, or a lower cost of living can be irresistible. Embracing the adventure of living abroad can be a transformative experience, but it's not without its challenges. This chapter dives into the stories of individuals who took the leap and successfully transitioned their lives to new countries. They faced various hurdles—language barriers, cultural differences, and even navigating unfamiliar legal and financial systems. But their experiences illustrate the rewards that come with embracing the unknown and forging a new path.

Emma, a young artist, traded the hustle of New York City for the artistic haven of Chiang Mai, Thailand. She had always been drawn to Southeast Asian culture and its vibrant art scene. The cost of living in Chiang Mai was significantly lower than in NYC, allowing her to dedicate more time and resources to her art. However, adjusting to a new culture wasn't easy. Emma learned to navigate the complexities of Thai customs, embraced the local language, and found a community of like-minded artists. The experience not only enriched her creative journey but also broadened her perspective on life.

John and Sarah, a retired couple from California, sought a more relaxed lifestyle in Portugal. They were tired of the hectic pace of life in the USA and longed for a slower, more affordable alternative. Portugal offered a welcoming environment for expats, with a lower cost of living and stunning natural beauty. They found a charming town in the Algarve region, where they spent their days exploring the coastline, enjoying the local cuisine, and connecting with the friendly locals. The challenges they faced included navigating the Portuguese healthcare system and learning the language, but their determination and positive attitude made the transition smooth.

Alex, a software engineer, was drawn to the tech hub of Berlin, Germany. He was seeking a change of scenery and a city with a strong tech industry. Berlin offered a dynamic and affordable lifestyle compared to many other major tech cities. Alex embraced the city's multicultural atmosphere, learned the German language, and found a supportive community of expats and locals. He discovered the city's vibrant nightlife, historical landmarks, and its progressive approach to technology. However, adapting to a new work environment and navigating the German bureaucracy required patience and persistence.

Emily, a single mother, decided to move to Costa Rica with her young daughter. She was seeking a safer, more affordable environment for her child and a lifestyle that prioritized nature and well-being. Costa Rica offered a peaceful and beautiful setting with excellent schools and affordable healthcare. They found a community of expats and locals who supported each other and created a sense of belonging. Emily embraced the slow pace of life, the fresh produce, and the opportunities for outdoor adventures. The challenges they faced included language barriers and the need to adapt to a different educational system. However, their resilience and positive spirit made the transition a success.

These are just a few examples of individuals who successfully navigated the challenges of living abroad. Their stories highlight the importance of adaptability, cultural sensitivity, and a willingness to learn. They also underscore the potential for growth, personal fulfillment, and financial benefits that come with embracing a new culture.

Here are some key takeaways from their experiences:

Research is crucial: Before making the move, thoroughly research the potential country, including its cost of living, healthcare system, legal requirements, and cultural norms.

Embrace cultural differences: Be open to different customs, traditions, and ways of life. Embrace the opportunity to learn and grow from new experiences.

Learn the language: Even a basic understanding of the local language can significantly ease your transition and make your daily interactions more enjoyable.

Build a support network: Connect with other expats, locals, and online communities to build a support system and find resources.

Stay adaptable: Be prepared to adjust your plans and expectations as you navigate new challenges and opportunities.

Seek out the benefits: Living abroad can offer unique opportunities for personal growth, career advancement, and financial stability. Focus on the positive aspects of your experience and enjoy the journey.

Moving abroad is a significant decision that requires careful planning and preparation. However, for those who are willing to embrace the challenges and rewards, it can be an enriching and fulfilling experience. These stories offer a glimpse into the diverse paths that individuals have taken to successfully navigate the transition, showcasing the power of determination, adaptability, and a sense of adventure.

Best Countries to Live as a US Expat

Nowadays, more Americans than ever are choosing to live abroad. Whether you're a solo digital nomad looking for your next place to post up, a family of four looking to start over on the other side of the world, or a retiree looking for a place to settle down, 2025 could be the perfect time to make the move. We've put together eight of the best countries to live as a US expat based on a mix of affordability, safety, quality of life, and career opportunities.

What Makes a Country Great for American Expats?

Here's a quick breakdown of the key stats we've used to determine what makes a country a best fit for US expats:

- **Cost of Living Index (CLI)**: A measure of affordability for everyday expenses such as groceries, rent, and transportation.
- **Quality of Life Index (QLI)**: A measure of overall well-being, which includes healthcare, commute times, and climate.
- **Global Peace Index (GPI)**: This index measures peacefulness and political stability.
- **Average Monthly Salary (USD)**: You can expect to earn this in your new host country.
- **Monthly Costs for Family (USD)**: Realistic cost of living expenses for a family, including food, utilities, transportation, and education.
- **Safety Index:** A score on perceived and statistical safety. The higher the score, the safer the country overall.

Outside of these parameters, you should also consider language barriers, the availability of visa types, and any tax implications (e.g., avoiding double taxation through tax treaties between the US and your host country).

Portugal

Portugal remains one of the most popular destinations for American expats, especially with digital nomads and retirees. Its mild Mediterranean climate, delicious food, affordable living, and comparatively simple visa programs make it an easy recommendation. Once outside Lisbon, expats can expect to find picturesque coastal cities and a laid-back pace of life. It's also ranked one of the safest countries in the world.

Quick Facts:

- **Cost of Living Index:** 44.56
- **Quality of Life Index:** 168.33
- **Global Peace Index Rank:** 7
- **Average Monthly Salary:** $2,500 – $4,000
- **Monthly Family Costs:** ~$2,676 (excluding rent)
- **Safety Index:** 68.8

Germany

Germany boasts a high standard of living, excellent healthcare, and strong economic opportunities. In major cities, expats have access to robust public transportation, vibrant food and beer culture, and a large English-speaking international community — especially in Berlin. For freelancers and digital nomads, Germany's generous working visas and tax treaties with the US make it a great base of operations in the heart of Europe.

Quick Facts:

- **Cost of Living Index:** 62.56
- **Quality of Life Index:** 192.29
- **Global Peace Index Rank:** 16
- **Average Monthly Salary:** ~$4,000
- **Monthly Family Costs:** ~$3,759 (excluding rent)
- **Safety Index:** 61.1

Spain

Spain continues to be another attractive country for US expats settling abroad. With its relative affordability, world-class cuisine, and year-round sunshine, Spain is a good choice for those looking to enjoy life at a slower pace. Spain's Non-Lucrative Visa allows non-EU residents, such as retirees and those with passive incomes, to remain in the country and potentially qualify for permanent residency after five years.

Quick Facts:

- **Cost of Living Index:** 53.77
- **Quality of Life Index:** 169.82
- **Global Peace Index Rank:** 29
- **Average Monthly Salary:** $1,800 – $2,200
- **Monthly Family Costs:** ~$2,500 (excluding rent)
- **Safety Index:** 63.8

Thailand

Thailand offers a tropical climate, excellent street food, and a vibrant expat community. Those looking to get out of urban areas can easily access beautiful beaches and mountains. Thailand's central location in Southeast Asia also makes it a great spot to hop around to nearby countries such as Vietnam, Laos, Taiwan, and Indonesia. With its low cost of living, Thailand is always a solid choice for expat retirees.

Quick Facts:

- **Cost of Living Index:** 40.7
- **Quality of Life Index:** 116.55
- **Global Peace Index Rank:** 103
- **Average Monthly Salary:** $800 – $1,000
- **Monthly Family Costs:** ~$2,000 (excluding rent)
- **Safety Index:** 42.3

Australia

Australia is an excellent choice for American expats who want something new and exotic but don't want to deal with a language barrier. With a high standard of living, multicultural society, and varied natural landscapes, Australia has much to offer families and retirees. Expats will also find access to excellent healthcare and education and safe and vibrant urban areas.

Quick Facts:

- **Cost of Living Index:** 73.54
- **Quality of Life Index:** 181.18
- **Global Peace Index Rank:** 22
- **Average Monthly Salary:** $3,000 – $4,200
- **Monthly Family Costs:** ~$3,800 (excluding rent)
- **Safety Index:** 57.2

New Zealand

Just a short plane ride away, New Zealand is famous for its breathtaking natural scenery, laid-back culture, and friendly locals. While housing prices can be a little steep in major cities, New Zealand's exceptionally low crime levels, education system, and universal healthcare make it the perfect place to raise a family.

Quick Facts:

- **Cost of Living Index:** 72.53
- **Quality of Life Index:** 187.96
- **Global Peace Index Rank:** 4
- **Average Monthly Salary:** ~$2,900
- **Monthly Family Costs:** ~$4,000 (excluding rent)
- **Safety Index:** 52.3

Austria

Often overlooked due to its small size, Austria has one of the highest quality of life in the world. Vienna, in particular, offers beautiful Baroque architecture, low crime, and a rich arts scene. Most of Austria is covered by the Alps and contains many freshwater lakes outside urban areas — including Lake Constance, one of the largest in Europe. Austria borders eight countries, and its central location makes it an excellent spot for getting around the rest of Europe.

Quick Facts:

- **Cost of Living Index:** 67.3
- **Quality of Life Index:** 190.4
- **Global Peace Index Rank:** 3
- **Average Monthly Salary:** ~$3,000 – $3,600

- **Monthly Family Costs:** ~$3,800 (excluding rent)
- **Safety Index:** 75.4

The Netherlands

The Netherlands offers safe and clean cities, high wages, and a great work-life balance. It is also home to numerous intentional schools, and its healthcare system consistently ranks as one of the best in the world. For those nervous about the language barrier, approximately 90–93% of the Dutch speak English.

Quick Facts:

- **Cost of Living Index:** 63.1
- **Quality of Life Index:** 207.5
- **Global Peace Index Rank:** 21
- **Average Monthly Salary:** ~$3,400
- **Monthly Family Costs:** ~$3,500 (excluding rent)
- **Safety Index:** 73.7

Final Thoughts

Packing everything up and moving to the other side of the world is never easy, but with proper research and planning, you can find a country that meets your needs. These are just a few suggestions for the best countries to live as a US expat out of many, and any country you choose will have its unique traits and come with its pros and cons.

As an American expat, you are responsible for reporting annual income and filing a tax return no matter where you go in the world. When researching countries, be sure to look for those that have tax treaties with the United States. This is the best way to avoid double taxation while abroad.

6

EMBRACING THE JOURNEY: TRAVEL AND LEISURE

The USA boasts a breathtaking array of natural wonders, and its national parks stand as testaments to the country's unparalleled beauty. From towering mountains to pristine beaches, from lush forests to arid deserts, each park offers a unique and unforgettable experience.

Let's embark on a journey to discover some of these iconic national parks, starting with the Grand Canyon National Park in Arizona. A testament to the erosive power of the Colorado River, the Grand Canyon is a geological masterpiece. Its immense scale and intricate layers of rock, dating back millions of years, evoke a sense of awe and wonder. Hike down to the river, or take a helicopter tour for a truly unforgettable perspective.

Next, venture to Yellowstone National Park in Wyoming, Montana, and Idaho. Here, geothermal activity comes alive in the form of geysers, hot springs, and mud pots. Old Faithful, the park's most famous geyser, erupts with predictable regularity, drawing crowds of eager spectators. Keep an eye out for wildlife, including bison, elk, wolves, and bears, roaming freely in their natural habitat.

In California, Yosemite National Park offers a different kind of grandeur. Towering granite cliffs like El Capitan and Half Dome are a sight to behold. Hike through meadows bursting with wildflowers, or challenge yourself with a challenging climb up to the summit of Half Dome. Yosemite Falls, cascading down the cliff face, is a breathtaking sight, especially during the spring melt.

The vast and rugged beauty of Glacier National Park in Montana is a sight to behold. Its pristine lakes, majestic peaks, and glaciers sculpted over millennia create a landscape straight out of a postcard. Go hiking through the forests, paddle across the lakes, or take a scenic drive along Going-to-the-Sun Road for panoramic views.

Journey to the Pacific Northwest to experience the serenity of Olympic National Park in Washington. Here, towering rainforests, rugged coastlines, and snow-capped mountains coexist in perfect harmony. Hike through old-growth forests, explore the tide pools along the rocky beaches, or climb to the summit of Hurricane Ridge for breathtaking views of the Olympic Mountains.

For those seeking adventure, Zion National Park in Utah is a must-visit. Zion Canyon is a narrow, steep gorge carved by the Virgin River, with towering sandstone cliffs.

Hike the Narrows, wading through the cool water of the Virgin River, or challenge yourself with the Angels Landing trail, a thrilling hike to a breathtaking viewpoint. The red rock formations of Arches National Park in Utah are a sight to behold. Over 2,000 natural sandstone arches, sculpted by wind and water erosion, create a surreal landscape. Hike to Delicate Arch, a symbol of the park, or explore the Double Arch, a unique and awe-inspiring formation.

Moving east, Shenandoah National Park in Virginia offers a different kind of natural beauty. The Blue Ridge Mountains, with their rolling hills and scenic overlooks, provide a peaceful retreat from the hustle and bustle of city life. Hike along the Appalachian Trail, drive the Skyline Drive for panoramic views, or explore the park's waterfalls and streams.

For a taste of the American Southwest, head to Big Bend National Park in Texas. Located on the border with Mexico, Big Bend is a vast, rugged landscape of mountains, deserts, and the Rio Grande River. Hike through the Chisos Mountains, explore the desert canyons, or go birding along the riverbanks.

While these are just a few of the many iconic national parks in the USA, they offer a glimpse into the country's vast and diverse natural beauty. Each park holds its own unique charm and offers unforgettable experiences for visitors of all ages and interests.

Beyond the national parks, the USA offers a wealth of affordable beach destinations for those seeking a relaxing getaway. From the sunny shores of Florida to the rugged coastlines of California, there's a beach for every taste and budget. Escape the crowds and explore the hidden gems of the Gulf Coast, where pristine beaches and charming towns offer a peaceful retreat.

For those looking for a more adventurous beach experience, the Pacific Northwest offers a rugged beauty with towering cliffs, crashing waves, and pristine beaches. Explore the tide pools, go kayaking or surfing, or simply relax on the sandy shores and soak up the fresh air.

Camping is an affordable and immersive way to experience the natural beauty of the USA. Whether you prefer roughing it in the wilderness or enjoying the amenities of a campground, there are countless options to choose from. For a true backcountry experience, head to the national parks and explore their designated campsites. For a more comfortable experience, opt for a campground with amenities like showers, restrooms, and fire pits.

Seasonal travel can be a smart way to save money and avoid crowds. During the shoulder seasons, spring and fall, you can often find lower prices on flights, hotels, and activities. Consider exploring destinations that are less popular during the peak season, or plan your trip around seasonal events like festivals or harvest festivals.

Balancing travel with financial goals is a key aspect of responsible travel. Set a realistic travel budget and stick to it. Look for affordable accommodation options, such as hostels, Airbnb rentals, or campgrounds. Take advantage of free activities, such as hiking, exploring parks, or visiting museums on free days. Plan your meals in advance and pack snacks to save money on eating out.

Remember, travel doesn't have to break the bank. With a little planning and creativity, you can explore the USA's iconic national parks, discover affordable beach destinations, and enjoy the great outdoors without sacrificing your financial well-being. Embracing the journey and experiencing the beauty of nature is a rewarding investment in your own happiness and well-being.

Have you ever dreamt of sinking your toes into the warm sand, feeling the salty breeze caress your skin, and watching the sun dip below the horizon, painting the sky in hues of orange and purple? We all crave those quintessential beach vacations, but the price tag can often deter us from making that dream a reality. Fear not, fellow wanderlusts, for there are hidden gems across the USA that offer all the beach bliss you could desire without breaking the bank.

Imagine this: waking up to the sound of crashing waves, sipping a cup of coffee on your balcony overlooking the ocean, and exploring vibrant coastal towns filled with charm and local flavors. This is the magic of affordable beach destinations, and the best part is, you don't have to sacrifice quality for affordability.

The Sunshine State's Affordable Shores: Florida is synonymous with beaches, but the state can also be surprisingly wallet-friendly, especially if you're willing to venture beyond the tourist-heavy hotspots. Consider Pensacola Beach, nestled on the panhandle. Known for its sugar-white sands and crystal-clear waters, Pensacola Beach offers a laid-back vibe, plenty of family-friendly activities, and a cost of living that won't drain your savings.

Embrace the Charm of the Carolina Coast: The Carolina coast boasts miles of unspoiled coastline, charming seaside towns, and a range of affordable beach destinations. Myrtle Beach, South Carolina, is a classic family-friendly choice with amusement parks, water parks, and endless miles of sandy shores. But if you're seeking a more tranquil escape, consider Outer Banks, North Carolina, where quaint fishing villages, historic lighthouses, and pristine beaches await.

California's Budget-Friendly Beaches: California may be known for its high cost of living, but a few budget-friendly beach destinations exist if you know where to look. Pismo Beach on the Central Coast offers a unique combination of stunning beaches, charming shops, and delicious seafood, all at a more affordable price point than its more glamorous neighbors.

The Undiscovered Gems of the Gulf Coast: The Gulf Coast, stretching from Texas to Florida, is a treasure trove of affordable beach destinations. Gulf Shores, Alabama, boasts pristine beaches, family-friendly attractions, and a laid-back atmosphere. If you're seeking a unique experience, consider South Padre Island, Texas, known for its vibrant nightlife, water sports, and proximity to the Rio Grande.

Beyond the Beach:

Coastal Towns and Adventures: While the beaches are undoubtedly the main attraction, these destinations offer much more. Explore charming coastal towns brimming with local history, art, and culture. Indulge in fresh seafood at charming seaside restaurants, savor the flavors of local breweries and wineries, and embark on exciting adventures like dolphin watching tours, kayaking expeditions, and fishing trips.

Tips for Saving Money on Your Beach Getaway:

Embrace the Off-Season: Travel during the shoulder seasons (spring and fall) to avoid crowds and enjoy lower prices on flights, accommodations, and attractions.

Consider Alternatives to Hotels: Choose vacation rentals, charming bed and breakfasts, or even campgrounds to save on lodging costs.

Pack Smart and Eat Like a Local: Avoid unnecessary luggage and pack light. Take advantage of local grocery stores and farmers' markets for budget-friendly meals. Embrace Free Activities: Enjoy the simple pleasures of the beach, such as swimming, sunbathing, building sandcastles, and collecting seashells. Explore free attractions like historical sites, art galleries, and nature trails.

Utilize Free Transportation: Consider walking, biking, or utilizing public transportation to avoid expensive parking fees and rental cars.

Planning Your Budget-Friendly Beach Escape:

Research and Compare: Compare prices for flights, accommodations, and activities online using travel search engines.

Set a Realistic Budget: Determine how much you're comfortable spending on your trip and allocate your budget accordingly.

Make Advance Bookings: Book your flights and accommodations in advance, especially during peak season, to secure the best deals.

Be Flexible with Dates: Consider traveling mid-week or during the shoulder seasons to find lower prices.

Utilize Discounts and Promotions: Look for discounts and promotional offers from airlines, hotels, and attractions.

Embrace a "Less is More" Mindset: Focus on experiences and quality time rather than lavish spending.

The True Reward:

Remember, the true reward of a beach vacation isn't just the stunning scenery or the luxurious amenities. It's the time you spend connecting with loved ones, creating lasting memories, and escaping the pressures of everyday life. These affordable beach destinations allow you to experience this magic without sacrificing your financial well-being. So, pack your bags, grab your sunscreen, and prepare to be enchanted by the beauty and affordability of the USA's hidden beach gems. Enjoy the journey, embrace the adventure, and let the soothing sounds of the ocean wash away your worries.

Camping has become a popular choice for those seeking an affordable and immersive way to experience nature's beauty. It offers a unique blend of adventure, relaxation, and connection with the outdoors, all while keeping your budget in check. With the right planning and equipment, camping can be a fulfilling experience for families, couples, and solo travelers alike.

The allure of camping lies in its simplicity and accessibility. Unlike extravagant vacations that involve expensive hotels and flights, camping allows you to disconnect from the hustle and bustle of everyday life and reconnect with nature. Imagine waking up to the sound of birds chirping, the smell of fresh pine, and the breathtaking sight of a sun-kissed landscape. You can choose to pitch your tent in a secluded forest, by a tranquil lake, or even on a rugged mountainside. The possibilities are endless.

One of the biggest advantages of camping is the cost-effectiveness. The upfront investment in camping gear may seem substantial, but it's an investment that pays off in the long run. You can enjoy multiple trips with the same equipment, making it a far more budget-friendly option than traditional vacations. Furthermore, camping allows you to control your spending. You can pack your own meals, snacks, and beverages, eliminating the need for expensive restaurant meals. You can even enjoy cooking over an open fire, adding a rustic charm to your experience.

Another compelling aspect of camping is the opportunity to experience the outdoors in its purest form. You can hike through scenic trails, swim in pristine lakes, stargaze under a canopy of stars, and immerse yourself in nature's tranquil embrace. This close connection with nature can be incredibly therapeutic, reducing stress and promoting mental well-being. Camping encourages you to embrace a slower pace of life, disconnecting from the digital world and fostering a sense of mindfulness.

Of course, camping isn't without its challenges. It requires some preparation, including choosing the right campsite, packing essential gear, and knowing how to set up camp. But with a little research and planning, these hurdles can be easily overcome.

Here are some tips to make your camping experience more enjoyable and hassle-free:

1. **Choosing the Right Campsite:**

Research and Plan: Before embarking on your camping trip, it's crucial to research and choose the right campsite. Consider your preferences, the type of camping experience you desire, and the amenities you need.

Campground Reservations: For popular campgrounds, especially during peak seasons, it's highly recommended to make reservations in advance. Many campgrounds allow online reservations through their websites or third-party booking platforms.

Campground Amenities: Think about the amenities you need or want. Some campgrounds offer basic amenities like restrooms and water sources, while others provide more luxurious options like showers, laundry facilities, and even electricity hookups.

Accessibility and Safety: Consider the accessibility of the campsite. If you have mobility challenges or are traveling with young children, ensure the campsite is accessible and safe. Also, consider safety factors like proximity to emergency services, wildlife encounters, and potential hazards.

2. **Essential Camping Gear:**

Tent: The tent is the heart of your campsite, so choosing the right one is essential. Consider the size of your group, the weather conditions you'll be camping in, and the type of terrain you'll be setting up on.

Sleeping Bags and Pads: Comfort is paramount during your camping adventure. Choose sleeping bags rated for the anticipated temperatures and sleeping pads for insulation and comfort.

Cooking Equipment: You'll need cooking equipment to prepare meals. A portable stove, cookware, utensils, a cooler for perishables, and a water container are essential items.

Lighting and Safety: Pack a flashlight, headlamp, lantern, and extra batteries. It's also wise to include first aid supplies, insect repellent, sunscreen, and a basic toolkit for repairs and maintenance.

3. **Packing for Comfort and Convenience:**

Clothing: Pack layers of clothing for various weather conditions, including a waterproof jacket, warm fleece, comfortable pants and shorts, and appropriate footwear for hiking.

Food and Water: Plan your meals and snacks in advance. Pack non-perishable items like canned goods, pasta, rice, granola bars, and trail mix. Remember to bring enough water for drinking and cooking.

Entertainment: Pack books, magazines, playing cards, or board games for entertainment. Consider a portable speaker for playing music or listening to podcasts.

4. **Campsite Safety and Hygiene:**

Fire Safety: Always be mindful of fire safety. Keep water nearby and ensure the fire is completely extinguished before leaving your campsite.

Food Storage: Securely store food and other scented items to prevent attracting wildlife. Use airtight containers and store them away from your tent.

Waste Management: Dispose of garbage properly. Use designated trash receptacles and pack out all your trash, leaving the campsite clean.

Leave No Trace: Adhere to the principles of Leave No Trace, minimizing your impact on the environment. Pack out all trash, dispose of waste properly, and avoid damaging vegetation or disturbing wildlife.

5. **Embrace the Experience:**

Disconnect and Unwind: Camping provides a great opportunity to disconnect from the digital world and reconnect with nature. Enjoy the sounds of the forest, the starlit sky, and the fresh air.

Explore Your Surroundings: Take advantage of the opportunity to explore the surrounding area. Go for hikes, swim in lakes or rivers, or simply enjoy the tranquility of nature.

Share Memories with Loved Ones: Camping offers a unique way to create lasting memories with loved ones. Share stories, play games, and enjoy the simple pleasures of nature together.

Top Camping Destinations in the USA

The United States boasts a diverse range of camping destinations, each offering a unique experience. From the towering peaks of the Rocky Mountains to the serene shores of the Pacific Ocean, you'll find countless campgrounds to choose from.

1. **Yellowstone National Park, Wyoming, Montana, and Idaho:** Yellowstone National Park is a UNESCO World Heritage Site known for its geothermal wonders, wildlife, and stunning

landscapes. It's home to geysers like Old Faithful, hot springs, canyons, and abundant wildlife, including wolves, bears, bison, and elk.

2. **Yosemite National Park, California:** Yosemite is a breathtaking wilderness area with towering granite cliffs, giant sequoia trees, cascading waterfalls, and diverse wildlife. It's a paradise for hikers, climbers, and nature enthusiasts.
3. **Grand Canyon National Park, Arizona:** The Grand Canyon is a geological wonder, with towering sandstone cliffs that create a breathtaking vista. It's a popular destination for hiking, mule riding, and simply marveling at the grandeur of nature.
4. **Acadia National Park, Maine:** Acadia National Park offers a rugged coastal experience with towering mountains, rocky shores, and abundant wildlife. It's known for its scenic drives, hiking trails, and picturesque lighthouses.
5. **Glacier National Park, Montana:** Glacier National Park is a pristine wilderness area with towering mountains, sparkling lakes, and glaciers. It's a paradise for hikers, backpackers, and nature photographers.
6. **Zion National Park, Utah:** Zion National Park is a popular destination for its dramatic sandstone cliffs, narrow canyons, and scenic hiking trails. It's a must-visit for those seeking adventure and stunning natural beauty.
7. **Olympic National Park, Washington:** Olympic National Park is a diverse park with old-growth

forests, rugged mountains, and pristine coastline. It's home to diverse wildlife, including bears, elk, and sea lions.

8. **Rocky Mountain National Park, Colorado:** Rocky Mountain National Park is a breathtaking wilderness area with alpine meadows, towering peaks, and abundant wildlife. It's known for its scenic drives, hiking trails, and opportunities for wildlife viewing.
9. **Great Smoky Mountains National Park, Tennessee and North Carolina:** The Great Smoky Mountains National Park is a stunning mountain range with lush forests, cascading waterfalls, and diverse wildlife. It's a popular destination for hiking, camping, and enjoying the beauty of nature.
10. **Sequoia and Kings Canyon National Parks, California:** Sequoia and Kings Canyon National Parks are home to giant sequoia trees, towering mountains, and deep canyons. It's a must-visit for those seeking to witness the grandeur of nature.

Tips for a Successful Camping Trip:

Check the Weather Forecast: Before embarking on your camping trip, check the weather forecast for the area you'll be visiting. Pack accordingly and be prepared for any potential changes in weather conditions.

Pack for All Seasons: Even if you're camping during a specific season, it's a good idea to pack for a range of weather conditions. Layer your clothing and bring items that can be used for both warm and cold weather.

Learn Basic Camping Skills: Before heading out, familiarize yourself with basic camping skills, including setting up your tent, starting a fire, and cooking over a campfire.

Be Prepared for Wildlife Encounters: Wildlife encounters are a part of the camping experience. Be aware of your surroundings, store food properly, and avoid leaving food or trash out in the open.

Leave No Trace: Practice the Leave No Trace principles to minimize your impact on the environment. Pack out all your trash, dispose of waste properly, and avoid damaging vegetation or disturbing wildlife.

Respect the Rules: Adhere to the campground rules and regulations to ensure a safe and enjoyable experience for everyone.

Have Fun: Camping is all about enjoying the outdoors and creating lasting memories. Relax, unwind, and embrace the beauty of nature.

Camping offers a unique and affordable way to experience nature's wonders. With careful planning and preparation, you can create lasting memories and connect with the great outdoors. From iconic national parks to secluded wilderness areas, the possibilities for outdoor adventures are endless. So, pack your bags, grab your gear, and embark on your next camping adventure.

The world is a vast tapestry of experiences waiting to be unraveled, and travel is the thread that connects us to its vibrant hues. But as we embark on these adventures, we often find ourselves tethered to the constraints of seasons. Winter brings snowy landscapes and cozy cabins, while summer beckons with sun-drenched beaches and bustling festivals. Recognizing these seasonal nuances can be a game-changer, transforming your travel plans from ordinary to extraordinary.

Imagine yourself strolling through a European city adorned with festive lights, the air thick with the scent of gingerbread and cinnamon. This magical scene unfolds during the holiday season, a time when charming Christmas markets and enchanting ice skating rinks enchant visitors. But to experience this winter wonderland, you need to plan ahead.

Similarly, if your heart desires the vibrant energy of a tropical paradise, summer is the time to embrace the sun-kissed shores and azure waters. But remember, summer also brings peak season crowds and inflated prices. So, how do you navigate the ebb and flow of seasonal changes and create travel experiences that are both enriching and budget-friendly?

The Art of Off-Season Exploration

The allure of peak season is undeniable, but it often comes with a hefty price tag. Travel costs, accommodation rates, and even the price of a simple cup of coffee can skyrocket during popular travel periods. The secret to unlocking affordable travel lies in embracing the off-season, a time when the world slows down, revealing its hidden charms.

Consider a journey to the breathtaking landscapes of Iceland during the shoulder seasons, spring and fall. While winter brings the mesmerizing Northern Lights, the shoulder seasons offer a unique perspective on this volcanic island. You'll encounter fewer crowds, experience more manageable weather conditions, and enjoy lower accommodation rates.

Traveling in the off-season also allows you to connect with local culture on a deeper level. With fewer tourists around, you have more opportunities to interact with locals, learn about their traditions, and savor the authentic flavors of their cuisine.

Embrace the Seasonal Celebrations

The world comes alive with vibrant festivals and celebrations throughout the year. From the colorful Holi festival in India to the lively Carnival celebrations in Rio de Janeiro, these events offer an unparalleled opportunity to immerse yourself in different cultures and create unforgettable memories.

Planning your trip around these seasonal events can elevate your travel experience, allowing you to witness the unique traditions and customs that define a region's identity. You'll be swept away by the infectious energy of local festivities, savor delicious regional cuisine, and create memories that will last a lifetime.

The Power of Flexibility

While planning ahead is essential, being flexible with your travel dates can unlock significant savings. The beauty of off-season travel lies in its ability to adapt to your budget and preferences. You can often find incredible deals on flights and accommodations by traveling during the weekdays or exploring alternative destinations that are less crowded.

Consider embracing the nomadic spirit and venturing off the beaten path. Discover lesser-known destinations that offer a more authentic and affordable travel experience. Explore charming towns, hidden beaches, or unique cultural experiences that lie outside the typical tourist circuit.

Strategies for Seasonal Travel

Now, let's dive deeper into practical strategies for planning seasonal travel that is both rewarding and financially responsible.

Research is Your Ally: Before embarking on your journey, take the time to research the destination's climate, seasonal events, and potential crowds. This information will guide you in choosing the best time to travel and maximizing your experience.

Embrace the Weather: Consider how the weather will affect your travel plans. Will you need warm clothing for winter adventures or a light wardrobe for summer escapades? Packing accordingly will ensure a comfortable and enjoyable experience.

Plan Around Festivals and Events: If you're seeking a festive atmosphere, plan your trip around local festivals and celebrations. Research online calendars for events in your chosen destination.

Look for Off-Peak Deals: Travel during the off-season or shoulder seasons to secure better deals on flights and accommodations. You can often find significant savings by booking in advance or taking advantage of last-minute deals.

Book Early for Popular Destinations: If you're planning to visit popular destinations during peak season, book your flights and accommodations well in advance. Prices tend to rise as the travel dates approach, and availability becomes limited.

Consider Alternative Transportation: Explore alternative transportation options like trains or buses, which can often be more affordable than flying, especially for shorter distances.

Embrace Local Experiences: Indulge in local cuisine, visit local markets, and interact with the people. This immersion will enrich your experience and help you discover the true spirit of the destination.

Stay in Local Accommodations: Instead of opting for luxury hotels, consider staying in guesthouses, apartments, or hostels. These options often offer a more authentic experience and can be significantly more affordable.

Be Prepared for Unexpected Changes: Keep in mind that unexpected changes can occur, especially with weather patterns. Pack a flexible itinerary and be open to adjusting your plans as needed.

Balancing Travel with Financial Goals

Travel shouldn't come at the expense of your financial well-being. It's about finding a balance between indulging in your travel desires and maintaining a healthy financial life. Here are some practical strategies:

Set a Travel Budget: Before you start planning, determine a realistic travel budget. This will help you stay on track and avoid overspending.

Save for Your Travels: Create a dedicated savings account for travel expenses. Set aside a portion of your income each month, no matter how small, to build up a travel fund.

Use Travel Rewards Credit Cards: Consider using travel rewards credit cards to earn points or miles that can be redeemed for flights, accommodations, or other travel expenses. However, remember to use them responsibly and pay off the balance in full each month.

Travel During Off-Peak Seasons: As mentioned earlier, traveling during the off-season or shoulder seasons can significantly reduce travel costs.

Explore Free or Affordable Activities: Seek out free or affordable activities in your destination. Take advantage of free walking tours, visit museums on free days, or explore parks and gardens.

Pack Light: Packing light can save you on baggage fees and make navigating airports and transportation easier.

Cook Some Meals: Consider cooking some of your own meals while traveling, especially if you're staying in a rental apartment or guesthouse.

By following these tips and strategies, you can embrace the journey of travel without compromising your financial goals. Remember, the true richness of travel lies not just in the destination but in the experiences you create along the way. Let the world be your canvas, and paint your memories with every adventure you embark upon.

The allure of travel is undeniable. It promises new experiences, broadened horizons, and a chance to escape the everyday grind. But for many, the cost of travel can be a significant barrier, especially when trying to balance it with other financial goals. The key lies in understanding that travel doesn't have to be an extravagant indulgence, but rather a rewarding experience that can be incorporated into a well-structured financial plan.

Strategic Planning for Affordable Adventures:

The first step towards responsible travel is strategic planning. This involves setting realistic budgets, exploring cost-effective options, and maximizing your travel dollars.

Instead of solely focusing on exotic destinations, consider exploring hidden gems closer to home or embracing off-season travel. Off-season travel often comes with lower flight and accommodation prices, allowing you to stretch your budget further.

Harnessing the Power of Rewards Programs:

Credit cards offering travel rewards programs can be a valuable asset. By strategically using these cards for everyday purchases and accumulating points, you can redeem them for flights, hotel stays, or even travel expenses. However, be mindful of interest rates and avoid accruing debt solely for travel rewards.

Accommodation Alternatives:

Hotels, while convenient, can quickly drain your travel budget. Explore alternative accommodation options like Airbnb, VRBO, or hostels to significantly reduce your expenses. These options offer a wider range of choices, often with unique local experiences and opportunities to connect with locals.

Embrace the Joy of Road Trips:

Road trips offer a budget-friendly way to explore new areas and experience the open road. Not only are fuel costs often lower than airfare, but you have the flexibility to stop at scenic overlooks, local attractions, and unique roadside diners along the way. Plan your route beforehand, pack snacks and drinks, and embrace the spontaneous nature of the journey.

Embrace Minimalism and Pack Smart:

Travel light! Overpacking adds unnecessary weight and often results in additional baggage fees. Pack efficiently, focusing on versatile clothing items that can be mixed and matched for various occasions. Avoid bringing unnecessary items that you can easily find at your destination.

Exploring Local Delights and Hidden Gems:

Local food markets, street vendors, and family-run restaurants often offer authentic culinary experiences at a fraction of the cost of tourist traps. Embrace the local culture and discover hidden gems that most tourists overlook. This not only saves you money but also provides a more authentic and enriching experience.

Harnessing Technology for Travel Savings:

Technology plays a crucial role in modern travel. Use travel apps to compare flight prices, find affordable accommodation options, and discover local attractions. These apps can help you identify deals and maximize your budget, ensuring you get the most out of your travel experience.

Travel Insurance for Peace of Mind:

While travel insurance can seem like an added expense, it offers valuable protection against unexpected events. From medical emergencies to flight delays, travel insurance can help mitigate financial risks and provide peace of mind while you explore the world.

The Art of Prioritization:

Balancing travel with financial goals involves prioritization. Determine what truly matters to you. Are you more interested in luxurious vacations or adventure-filled journeys? Do you prioritize exploring new cultures or immersing yourself in the natural world? Once you understand your travel priorities, you can allocate your resources accordingly.

Financial Discipline and Long-Term Goals:

Maintaining financial discipline is essential for travel enthusiasts. Create a budget that incorporates your travel goals while still allowing for savings, debt repayment, and other financial priorities. Remember that responsible travel is about striking a balance between fulfilling your travel desires and maintaining financial stability.

Embracing the Journey:

Travel is a journey, not just a destination. The memories and experiences you gather along the way are often more valuable than the physical destination itself. Embrace the journey, savor the moments, and remember that the most enriching travels are those that align with your personal values and financial goals.

Case Study: The Digital Nomad Couple:

Sarah and Mark, a young couple, embraced the digital nomad lifestyle. They both worked remotely, allowing them to travel the world while managing their finances responsibly. They carefully researched destinations with a lower cost of living, like Southeast Asia, and found affordable accommodation options. They used free Wi-Fi at cafes and co-working spaces, minimizing their expenses. Sarah and Mark learned to cook simple meals, explored local markets for fresh produce, and prioritized experiences over material possessions. This approach enabled them to travel extensively while maintaining their financial stability, proving that travel can be a sustainable and rewarding part of a well-structured financial plan.

Case Study: The Retired Adventurer

John, a retired engineer, always dreamed of exploring the world. After years of careful saving, he decided to embark on a year-long adventure. He researched destinations offering a combination of cultural immersion and affordable living, like South America. He learned Spanish, embraced local customs, and found joy in simple pleasures, such as exploring nature and connecting with

locals. John's responsible travel plan, based on research, budgeting, and adaptability, allowed him to fulfill his travel dreams while maintaining his financial well-being.

Travel is a Reflection of Your Values

In conclusion, travel is a reflection of your values and priorities. It should align with your financial goals and enhance your overall well-being. By prioritizing experiences over possessions, embracing alternative options, and utilizing technology wisely, you can make travel a fulfilling and financially responsible part of your life. Remember, responsible travel is about finding the sweet spot between exploring the world and maintaining financial stability, allowing you to embark on unforgettable adventures while making informed and sustainable decisions.

LAST WORD FROM THE AUTHOR

"Here's to the Crazy Ones:

The misfits. The rebels. The troublemakers. The round pegs in the square holes. The ones who see things differently. They're not fond of rules. And they have no respect for the status quo. You can quote them, disagree with them, glorify or vilify them. About the only thing you can't do is ignore them. Because they change things. They push the human race forward. And while some may see them as the crazy ones, we see genius. Because the people who are crazy enough to think they can change the world, are the ones who do."

Possessions can be a burden—they consume our energy and attention.

We give ourselves away to them. So when we free ourselves of them, we feel liberated. We feel like we've regained and reconnected with our authentic selves.The idea that wealth brings well-being also stops us from focusing on the real sources of happiness, such as flow, contact with nature, relationships, and inner harmony. These are much more reliable and productive sources of well-being. They offer stable and authentic well-being, materialism only offers short bursts of pleasure, which fade quickly. My wife often reminds me a hearst does not tow a U-haul.

BACK MATTER

I am deeply grateful to the many individuals who have contributed to the creation of this book. Their insights, support, and encouragement have been invaluable throughout the writing process.

First and foremost, I would like to express my sincere gratitude to the ones that dared to go against the grain, their unwavering belief in this project and their invaluable guidance.

I am also indebted to my wife for her thoughtful reviews and constructive feedback. Her sharp eyes and insightful comments helped me to refine my arguments and improve the clarity of my writing.

Special thanks to my friends, for sharing their personal stories and experiences, which bring to life the real-life implications of the topics explored in this book.

Finally, I would like to thank my family and friends for their unwavering support and understanding during the long hours spent writing. Their encouragement and love have made this journey possible. Their "joie de vie" provided me with a strong foundation for the book. Life comes with so many choices. The question remains: Is happiness the answer?

ABOUT THE AUTHOR

Gabriel Palotas is an internationally recognized real estate broker with over 30 years of experience. A true veteran of the industry, he was instrumental in introducing Buyer's Agency to Remax and has successfully managed multiple real estate offices.

In recognition of his dedication and concern for the community, the City of Fort Lauderdale officially proclaimed December 13, 2001, as Palotas Day. As a former Economic Chairman for the City of Fort Lauderdale, he has spent his career addressing common real estate challenges, earning millions of fans in the process.

With a belief that success comes from experience—including its failures—Palotas combines humility and a flexible approach to navigate the ever-changing real estate landscape. He holds a degree from Sir George University and is also a certified auctioneer. His expertise has not only led to numerous accolades but also established him as a trusted voice in the world of real estate.

www.ingramcontent.com/pod-product-compliance
Lightning Source LLC
LaVergne TN
LVHW022207200926
848481LV00006B/1881
* 9 7 9 8 8 9 9 5 0 3 2 0 7 *